INTERNATIONAL AND FOREIGN LEGAL RESEARCH

IN A NUTSHELL®

FOURTH EDITION

MARCI B. HOFFMAN
Associate Law Librarian (Emerita)
University of California,
Berkeley School of Law

WEST ACADEMIC

860 Blue Gentian Road, Suite 350
Eagan, MN 55121
1-877-888-1330

Published in the United States of America

ISBN: 979-8-89209-700-0

PREFACE

This *Nutshell* is designed for the international and foreign legal research novice. I finished this edition in August 2024. I mention the date because things keep changing and knowing the date when any source was created or updated is crucial.

Some people believe that all international and foreign law is now available for free on the web. Other people believe that the truth of international law lies only in the dusty volumes on a library shelf. I fall somewhere in between. My goal is to discuss the best sources. I have focused on the print and electronic sources that are the most important, regardless of format. Most of the sources that I discuss are readily available to anyone with access to a law library or the web, preferably both. However, this *Nutshell* will no doubt leave some researchers wanting more or needing more in-depth research assistance. I suggest chatting with a law librarian about your specific research issue or checking out some of the books and other sources that I suggest which go into much greater detail.

Comments and suggestions should be directed to Marci Hoffman (mhoffman@berkeley.edu).

ACKNOWLEDGMENTS

I am working on this edition shortly into my retirement after having worked for nearly thirty-five years as a law librarian and legal research instructor. I want to thank all the students, faculty, researchers, and colleagues who asked me questions and took my class for over three decades. I wouldn't know as much about international and foreign legal research if you all hadn't taken an interest and posed interesting research problems and questions.

A big thanks goes out to Kristie Chamorro, Instructional & Educational Technology Librarian at the Berkeley Law Library. Without her help, I would have been lost in the world of legal AI tools.

Finally, I also wish to thank Jay Miller for tolerating my long hours working and preparing to teach for more than three decades. Your constant support and cooking/baking skills kept me going throughout my career. Plus, brownies on the first day of class always made me a better instructor.

ABBREVIATIONS AND ACRONYMS

ABA	American Bar Association
ASIL	American Society of International Law
CJEU	Court of Justice of the European Union
COE	Council of Europe
C.T.S.	*Consolidated Treaty Series*
EC	European Community
ECHR	European Convention on Human Rights
ECtHR	European Court of Human Rights
ECJ	Court of Justice of the European Union
ECOSOC	United Nations Economic and Social Council
ECSC	European Coal and Steel Community
EEC	European Economic Community
EU	European Union
EURATOM	European Atomic Energy Community

FALM	Free Access to Law Movement
FAO	Food and Agriculture Organization
GATT	General Agreement on Trade and Tariffs
GenAI	Generative Artificial Intelligence
IACtHR	Inter-American Court of Human Rights
ICAO	International Civil Aviation Organization
ICC	International Criminal Court
ICJ	International Court of Justice
ICRC	International Committee of the Red Cross
ICSID	International Center of Settlement of Investment Disputes
ICTR	International Criminal Tribunal for Rwanda
ICTY	International Criminal Tribunal for the former Yugoslavia
IGO	intergovernmental organization

ILC	International Law Commission
ILO	International Labor Organization
IMF	International Monetary Fund
IMO	International Maritime Organization
IRMCT	International Residual Mechanism for Criminal Tribunals
ITLOS	International Tribunal for the Law of the Sea
LII	Legal Information Institute
L.N.T.S.	*League of Nations Treaty Series*
LSN	Legal Scholarship Network
NGO	nongovernmental organization
OAS	Organization of America States
OCLC	Online Computer Library Center
ODS	Official Document System of the United Nations
OECD	Organization for Economic Co-operation and Development

OHCHR	Office of High Commissioner for Human Rights
PCA	Permanent Court of Arbitration
PCIJ	Permanent Court of International Justice
RSS	Really Simple Syndication, Rich Site Service
SSRN	Social Science Research Network
TEU	Treaty on European Union
T.I.A.S.	*Treaties and Other International Acts Series*
TIF	Treaties in Force
TRIPs	Agreement on Trade-Related Aspects of Intellectual Property Rights
U.K.	United Kingdom
UN	United Nations
UNCTAD	United Nations Conference on Trade and Development
UNESCO	United Nations Education, Scientific and Cultural Organization
UNHCR	United Nations High Commissioner for Refugees
UNODC	United Nations Office on Drugs and Crime

U.N.T.S.	*United Nations Treaty Series*
UPU	Universal Postal Union
U.S.	United States
U.S.T.	*United States Treaties and Other International Agreements*
WHO	World Health Organization
WIPO	World Intellectual Property Organization
WTO	World Trade Organization

OUTLINE

INTERNATIONAL AND FOREIGN LEGAL RESEARCH

IN A NUTSHELL®

FOURTH EDITION

CHAPTER 1

INTRODUCTION AND BASIC CONCEPTS

1.1 INTRODUCTION

The study of international law is quite ancient. So long as ships have sailed the seas and nations have traded, warred, and made agreements, there has been a need for international law. Because there is no governing power that stands above the nations of the world, international law has developed over time as a series of compromises. Thus, international law is much blurrier around the edges than the law of any nation.

Until recently, the practice of international law has been the province of specialists. A small, and quite often scholarly, subset of the general practice of law, these lawyers and scholars formed an identifiable community. Most law schools offered a course or two that covered some part of international law, but such offerings were never part of the main curriculum.

In the past few decades, the role of international law (not to mention comparative law) has changed dramatically. The increasing pace of globalization has moved international and comparative law to center stage. Some law schools have integrated international or transnational features into their curricula by adding components to the regular first-year courses; some now require a specialized course on transnational or international law; and more and more schools are offering a wide range of classes on international topics. Even a lawyer who intends to spend her life practicing law in her home state will find international issues impinging on her work. These developments combine to make basic international legal research a necessary skill for every lawyer. The need for this *Nutshell* grows every day.

Researching international, foreign, comparative, or transnational law requires a basic understanding of some key concepts before delving into the sources. Many terms employed in international, foreign, and comparative research are used interchangeably, and in the past, have been used sloppily. Before beginning your research, you will need to understand a bit of background about what you are doing. This *Nutshell* will focus primarily on researching international law, but there is also coverage of foreign and comparative law research. Before getting started, some basic definitions are necessary, so you understand these terms as they are used throughout this *Nutshell*.

Along with some basic concepts, this *Nutshell* references primary sources and secondary sources throughout. Primary sources contain the law itself and secondary sources are usually analysis, commentary, or research tools. Books, journal articles, and reports are all considered secondary sources.

1.2 BASIC CONCEPTS

A. PUBLIC INTERNATIONAL LAW

Public international law governs the relationships between national governments, the relationships between intergovernmental organizations, and the relationships between national governments and intergovernmental organizations. It regulates governments and intergovernmental organizations across national boundaries. In the older world of international law, before the development of world markets and the dizzying variety of international and transnational bodies of today, public international law was the primary focus of research. While it is still important, today it is only the beginning.

Public international law seeks to address a variety of issues, but the most common are human rights, international trade, international environmental law, intellectual property, and arbitration. In the end, most of these topics revolve around treaties as the primary body of law, but they also include the work of international organizations, both intergovernmental and nongovernmental.

B. PRIVATE INTERNATIONAL LAW

Private international law governs the choice of law when there are conflicts in the domestic law of different countries that relate to private transactions between individual parties. In the U.S., Canada, and England, this general area is known as conflict of laws. National laws are the primary sources of private international law. However, private international law is also embodied in public international law sources, especially treaties and conventions (for example, the aptly named Hague Conventions on Private International Law[1]). There is really no well-defined body of private international law. You will find it lurking everywhere.

Private international law deals with topics such as contracts, marriage and divorce, jurisdiction, recognition of judgments, and child adoption and abduction. These areas can reach into the life of the solo practitioner no matter where they practice law.

C. FOREIGN LAW

Foreign law is essentially the national or sub-national law of a sovereign nation. It defines the role of governments with relation to the people they govern and controls relationships between people. It may regulate foreign persons and entities when they

1 https://www.hcch.net/en/instruments/conventions.

are within the borders of the national entity, but it does not have effect outside the boundaries of a nation. Foreign law is embodied in constitutions, statutes, regulations, and court decisions. Constitutions, statutes, and regulations are primary sources of law for all jurisdictions. Court decisions are also primary sources of law in common law jurisdictions, but they are considered secondary sources of law in civil law jurisdictions. If you need to know the law in France on a certain topic (and you are not French), then you will be consulting foreign law.

Many nations have well-organized systems for publishing their laws, but such sources appear in the language of that country. Some nations have more basic or convoluted systems of publishing law. No one said that this was going to be easy.

There are five legal systems in the world today: civil law, common law, customary law, religious law, and mixed legal systems. Until recently, one would have listed communist law as a separate system, but with Vietnam and China looking more and more like mixed systems based in civil law, only North Korea can claim a truly communist ideology, and its legal system is sui generis. Many systems are mixed because two or more legal systems are applied within the jurisdiction.

For a quick look at the major legal systems (civil law, common law, etc.), see JuriGlobe-World Legal

Systems.[2] It provides a bit of background, it is on the web, and it is free. What could be better?

D. COMPARATIVE LAW

Comparative law is "the study of the similarities and differences between the laws of two or more countries, or between two or more legal systems. Comparative law is not itself a system of law or a body of rules, but rather a method or approach to legal inquiry."[3]

Therefore, the most useful sources are books and articles that focus on the comparison of national law or legal systems. Comparative law is largely the turf of scholars and academics, and it seldom has an application in the practice of law. It is mysterious to many American legal researchers because it often calls for the mastery of more than one language, and mastery at a very sophisticated level. However, Professor Alan Watson has said, "[c]omparative law provides unique insights into law in general, the forces behind legal change, law and society."[4] For more background information, see *The Cambridge Companion to Comparative Law* (Mauro Bussani & Ugo Mattei, eds., 2012), *Oxford Handbook of Comparative Law* (Mathias Reimann & Rienhard Zimmermann, eds.) (2nd ed. 2019), Mary Ann Glendon, *Comparative Legal Traditions in a Nutshell*

---

[2] https://www.juriglobe.ca/.

[3] Robert C. Berring et al., *How to Find the Law* 565 (9th ed. 1989).

[4] Alan Watson, *Comparative Law: Law, Reality and Society*, see Preface (3rd ed. 2010).

(4th ed. 2016), and Alan Watson, *Comparative Law: Law, Reality and Society* (3rd ed. 2010).

E. TRANSNATIONAL LAW

Transnational law generally includes "all law which regulates actions or events that transcend national frontiers. Both public and private international law are included, as are other rules which do not wholly fit into such standard categories."[5] Furthermore, "works on this subject invariably focus on the legal relationship between a person and alien individuals or corporations, most frequently in commercial, industrial or investment situations."[6] Transnational law has been the locus of much of the growth in international practice. It is a field that is defining itself as the world shrinks due to globalization.

Transnational law is another term that is hard to pin down. When you encounter it, it will most likely lead to one of the other sources. Remember, these are areas of research that lack hard and fast boundaries.

F. SOFT LAW

Soft law encompasses non-binding documents or instruments (such as guidelines, declarations, and principles) that may be politically significant but that are not enforceable. Not that any international law is really enforceable, but soft law does not even have

---

5 Philip C. Jessup, *Transnational Law* 2 (1956).

6 *Parry and Grant Encyclopaedic Dictionary of International Law* 612 (3rd ed. 2009).

the pretense of being more than aspirational. Soft law has been effective in international economic law and international environmental law and is often created by international organizations.

Some examples of soft law include "Norms on the Responsibilities of Transnational Corporations and Other Business Enterprises with Regard to Human Rights"[7] or the Food and Agriculture Organization's (FAO) *Code of Conduct for Responsible Fisheries* (1995). For more information on soft law, see Daniel Thürer, *Soft Law*.[8]

G. SUPRANATIONAL LAW

Practically speaking, there is only one supranational legal order—the European Union (EU). At the time that this book is being updated, 2024, the EU has gone through Brexit and continues to evolve in the international community, but it remains an important international organization. A supranational organization has the following characteristics: (1) it has powers that its member states do not have because they surrendered those powers to it; (2) it may enact rules that preempt the laws and regulations of its member states; and (3) it can grant rights and privileges to the nationals of its member states, which those nationals may directly invoke.

---

[7] UN Doc. E/CN.4/Sub.2/2003/12/Rev.2, https://digitallibrary.un.org/record/501576?ln=en&v=pdf.

[8] Daniel Thürer, "Soft Law," *Max Planck Encyclopedias of International Law* (2009), https://opil.ouplaw.com/home (subscription database).

The EU is a highly articulated and complex organization that will enter into the discussion at many points throughout this *Nutshell*. The various components of the EU generate many terms and concepts that will be used throughout this book. By no means do I hope to cover all the terminology encountered when doing research in this area. Indeed, much of the study of international and foreign legal systems is laden with unfamiliar terms. To alleviate this problem, I will outline some background sources in Chapter 2. But this is a *Nutshell*, so it will use a very broad brush to paint a very complicated picture.

1.3 SOURCES OF LAW

One of the keys to understanding international and foreign legal materials is recognizing that there is no single source of authority to which you can turn. Describing the sources of law in a single legal system is much more straightforward than trying to do the same for all other systems, to say nothing of the world of international law. Because each nation is a sovereign entity, it possesses primary and secondary sources of law. This means that some sources have binding authority, some are considered persuasive, and others are used to locate binding and persuasive authority.

Even more important, each nation has the power to enforce its laws. If it is to remain sovereign, it must have control of its people and its territory, and its laws must be binding. Such national law is embodied in constitutions, statutes, regulations, and court decisions—primary sources of law for all jurisdictions. Court decisions are also primary sources of law in common law jurisdictions, but they are considered secondary sources of law in civil law jurisdictions. In later chapters, I will show you how to get a basic grasp of how the system of each nation works. You will find that lots of help awaits you.

Customary law plays a role in some legal systems, though no country operates solely under a customary law system. Customary law tends to govern areas of personal conduct, inheritance, and marriage. Most often, customary law is unwritten and is dispensed by persons with elected or hereditary roles within a community. In practice, it functions similarly to the common law that undergirds the judicial opinions of American and English courts.

The sources of public international law lack the same sovereign power as the sources of national law. There is no central authority and no ability to make public international law stick. It is true that nations can work together to punish a rogue nation or to enforce a norm, but these are ad hoc occurrences and not part of a system. Sometimes nations combine as rogues to violate established norms. The world is far from simple. Thus, the sources of public international law are always subject to dispute and interpretation. This does not mean that they are not important, but it does mean that they must be viewed in context.

The traditional sources of public international law are listed below. Their authority is based on Article 38 of the International Court of Justice Statute (the

ICJ Statute),[9] which is "generally considered to be the most authoritative enumeration of the sources of international law."[10]

- International conventions (treaties);
- Customary law (the general practices of States and intergovernmental organizations that are legally binding and generally recognized by all States);
- General principles of law; and
- Judicial decisions and the teachings of the most highly qualified publicists of the various nations.

For a more detailed analysis of the sources of international law, see *The Oxford Handbook of the Sources of International Law* (Samantha Besson & Jean d'Aspremont, eds., 2018).

To provide you with a ground-level view of how the different legal systems use authority, I refer you to the chart set out below.

---

9 https://www.icj-cij.org/statute.

10 Thomas Buergenthal & Sean D. Murphy, *Public International Law in a Nutshell* 22 (6th ed. 2019).

	Common Law	Civil Law	Public International Law	Private International Law
Primary Sources	Constitutions	Constitutions	Treaties	National Law
	Statutes/ Codes	Statutes/ Codes	Customary Law	Treaties
	Regulations	Regulations	Generally Recognized Principles of Law	Customary Law
	Court Decisions			
Secondary Sources	Scholarly Commentary	Court Decisions (jurisprudence)*	Court Decisions	Court Decisions
		Scholarly Commentary*	Teachings of Publicists (Scholarly Commentary)	Scholarly Commentary

* These authorities have weight when primary sources are absent or unclear; they are never binding.

1.4 TYPES OF LEGAL SOURCES

Researching international and foreign law requires that you look at a variety of sources for law and for commentary. You will encounter tools that are not familiar parts of the usual American legal research problem. The sources of law and secondary materials will be available in many different print and electronic sources. Though some may look quite different than what you are accustomed to using, there are more similarities than differences. Throughout this *Nutshell*, you will learn about many types of legal materials, including books, documents, commercial databases, freely available websites, journal articles, and people. Research in international law is becoming more straightforward every day. This is a good thing because if you are a law student or young lawyer reading this chapter, international and foreign legal questions will find you.

CHAPTER 2
SOME BASICS AS YOU BEGIN

2.1 INTRODUCTION

If you are new to international and foreign legal research, you will not get very far before you encounter something confusing. Many terms, phrases, and abbreviations used in international law are unfamiliar to the typical U.S. researcher. The good news is that just as with the abbreviations that appear in American legal materials, you do not have to memorize every one of them. The skill you need is the ability to look up what an abbreviation means. The following sources may be useful for finding definitions and for deciphering the alphabet soup of international organizations and materials. For a good source to check for updates on these tools, see the Berkeley Law Library research guide, "Basic & Background Sources for International & Foreign Legal Research."[1]

[1] https://libguides.law.berkeley.edu/c.php?g=326623.

2.2 ABBREVIATIONS AND CITATIONS

Some of the standard tools useful for deciphering American legal abbreviations can also prove useful for international legal abbreviations. One such tool is Julie Roberts Furgerson, *Prince's Dictionary of Legal Abbreviations: A Reference Guide for Attorneys, Legal Secretaries, Paralegals, and Law Students* (10th ed. 2021). This source, often used by experienced researchers, is a goldmine. It is the tool that the professionals use first, so you should use it, too.

A few abbreviation guides are geared toward citations specific to international and foreign law. One good guide is Igor I. Kavass, *World Dictionary of Legal Abbreviations* (1991–). This multivolume set is arranged by language and by subject. For special help when it comes to understanding citations to case reporters from other jurisdictions and from international courts, see *Noble's Revised International Guide to the Law Reports* (2002). Donald Raistrick, *Index to Legal Citations and Abbreviations* (4th ed. 2013), is helpful when working with European abbreviations. One of the more pleasant features of abbreviations is that they usually stay the same over time, so even a dated source can be of help.

The most comprehensive website for abbreviations is the Cardiff Index to Legal Abbreviations.[2] This index mainly focuses on abbreviations from English-language legal publications from the British Isles, the Commonwealth, and the U.S. However, it

---

2 http://www.legalabbrevs.cardiff.ac.uk/.

includes abbreviations covering international and comparative law sources. This site is simple to use, and it is free, but it is now a bit dated. If you remain a fan of books, a guide for abbreviations by foreign jurisdiction is the *International Citator and Research Guide: The Greenbook* (2018–). Six volumes are planned, one on international organizations, and the rest covering countries by regions.

Questions about proper citation format come to the reference desk weekly. Many researchers find *The Bluebook* difficult to use or lacking information for specific jurisdictions and certain types of documents (although it is pretty good for documents from major international organizations). There are other citation guides available that can be useful for figuring out how to cite to law from another jurisdiction and for figuring out some of those puzzling abbreviations (in addition to those mentioned above).

- *Australian Guide to Legal Citation* (4th ed. 2018).[3]
- *Canadian Guide to Uniform Legal Citation = Manuel Canadien de la Référence Juridique* (10th ed. 2023). Also available on Westlaw Canada.
- International Citation Manual.[4]
- *Guide to Foreign and International Legal Citations* (2nd ed. 2009).

---

3 http://law.unimelb.edu.au/mulr/aglc/about.

4 https://apps.law.wustl.edu/gslr/icm.html.

- OSCOLA: Oxford University Standard for the Citation of Legal Authorities (4th ed. 2012).[5]

2.3 DICTIONARIES AND ENCYCLOPEDIAS

Dictionaries and encyclopedias help the researcher locate definitions and general descriptions of international and foreign legal terms and concepts. They can provide necessary context and background when one is working in an unfamiliar area. Remember that knowing the terrain is vital. Even elementary background sources can be a huge help. The very best source for information on international law is the *Max Planck Encyclopedias of International Law* (2012–).[6] This set provides a fairly complete analysis of many international law concepts and subjects. It is readable, straightforward, and can be a real lifesaver. Other useful, yet less extensive, works include *Parry & Grant Encyclopaedic Dictionary of International Law* (3rd ed. 2009).[7] The latter two sources are commonly found in academic law libraries.

There are three additional dictionaries that can offer basic help. They are James R. Fox, *Dictionary of*

---

[5] https://www.law.ox.ac.uk/oscola.

[6] Available online at https://opil.ouplaw.com/home/EPIL (subscription database). This source includes the *Max Planck Encyclopedia of Public International Law*, as well as the *Max Planck Encyclopedia of International Procedural Law*. While the *Encyclopedia of Public International Law* is available in print, it the content has not been updated.

[7] Also available online at https://www.oxfordreference.com (subscription database) Unfortunately, the electronic version is no more current than the print edition.

International and Comparative Law (3rd ed. 2003), Boleslaw A. Boczek, *International Law: A Dictionary* (2005), and Curtis F.J. Doebbler, *Dictionary of Public International Law* (2018).

While there are many web-based dictionaries, there are few reliable and authoritative legal dictionaries to be found free in cyberspace and, unfortunately, really nothing that focuses on international law. This will likely change, but for now, to quote the great wise woman: it is what it is. Try a book.

Help with context, definitions, and basic explanations can be found in the *Restatement of the Law, Third and Fourth, the Foreign Relations Law of the United States* (2018, annual supplements).[8] Like other elements in the *Restatement* series, these volumes provide a comprehensible structure with excellent content and a plethora of cross-references. This is a good source for getting an understanding of the basic doctrines of international law from a U.S. perspective. The *Restatements* are produced under the auspices of the American Law Institute and reflect the best thinking of American lawyers, judges, and academics. It is a powerful, persuasive source that works hard to explain itself.

---

[8] Also available on Lexis, Westlaw, and HeinOnline (subscription databases). The Fourth has not revised Third in its entirety and researchers need to use both.

2.4 RESEARCH GUIDES

One of the most important tenets of carrying out efficient legal research is to find someone who has done the work for you. No matter what research problem one encounters, it is likely that someone has worked on it before. The people who work in the international and comparative legal research community have a true egalitarian spirit, and many have tried to leave a map for those who follow. For example, many international law librarians and lawyers create research guides that focus on a particular topic or jurisdiction. By using these guides, the novice (and sometimes even the expert) researcher can locate both print and electronic sources quickly and efficiently.

GlobaLex is a useful collection of research guides covering a variety of international law topics and foreign jurisdictions.[9] GlobaLex contains guides prepared by law librarians and lawyers from around the world. Some are done from the perspective of academic law librarians; some are focused on questions closer to the practice of law. Since many librarians post guides on library websites, more guides can be located by searching the web for the topic or jurisdiction (or region) and the phrase "legal research guide." The researcher who finds a research guide has a leg up on any research problem. Other useful guides include:

---

[9] https://www.nyulawglobal.org/globalex.

Guide to International Legal Research (annual)[10] provides a solid basis from which to start research for both international legal topics and selected foreign legal jurisdictions.

Foreign Law Guide[11] covers many jurisdictions and is the best source for locating foreign law. You will hear much more about this resource elsewhere in the *Nutshell.*

2.5 DIRECTORIES

Most intergovernmental organizations and non-governmental organizations have websites. These sites provide information about the organizations and usually contain documents and reports created by the various bodies. As with everything else on the internet, the quality depends on the source who produces the website. Often, a Google search using the name of the organization will yield a link to the relevant website, as will a search using the acronym for the organization. In the event you need a more organized approach, directories should not be ignored (really). They can provide descriptive information on a wide range of organizations, particularly by subject or geographic region. The best directories include the Associations Unlimited database; Europa World

---

10 Also available on Lexis+ and the LexisNexis Digital Library.

11 https://referenceworks.brill.com/display/db/flg (subscription database).

database; and the *Yearbook of International Organizations* (1967–).[12]

2.6 CLASSICS

International law has been around for centuries. Because of this long history, and because of the fact that international legal norms cross boundaries and lack a central authority, the writings of scholars take on an importance that goes beyond anything that exists in the American system. The closest analogy would be the influence on federal civil procedure exerted by *Federal Practice and Procedure* (Wright & Miller), but even that is based on interpreting underlying legislation. When it comes to the influential works on international law, there is a special kind of personal authority. Of course, the original author of the work may be long gone, but the prestige carries on. The researcher can use these works for background, for research guidance, or to construct persuasive arguments.

There are many classic works in international law, and these are good places for the novice to get familiar with the framework of this topic. Some of the most highly regarded include Ian Brownlie, *Principles of Public International Law* (9th ed. 2019); *Oppenheim's International Law: United Nations* (Rosalyn Higgins et al., 2017); Peter Malanczuk, *Akehurst's Modern Introduction to International Law* (8th ed. 2019); and Malcolm Shaw, *International Law* (9th ed. 2021). A good collection of works is available

---

[12] All of these are available electronically by subscription; check with a librarian or check Appendix A for websites.

on Oxford's Scholarly Authorities on International Law (OSAIL) database.[13] This collection covers over 180 classic titles published by Oxford University Press. While there is no comprehensive list of these classic works, the following sources list many of these titles: Oxford Bibliographies: International Law,[14] and HeinOnline's Legal Classics: International Law.[15]

The United Nations (with the support of HeinOnline) provides a freely available collection of scholarly writings on a variety of international law topics. This collection, called the Audiovisual Library of International Law, includes works from some of the most important international law scholars, like Ian Brownlie, Hersch Lauterpacht, and others.[16]

If you are unsure, ask your professor or a librarian about what is considered a classic in the field in which you are working.

---

13 https://opil.ouplaw.com/home/OSAIL (subscription database).

14 https://www.oxfordbibliographies.com/ (subscription database). For a quick overview of the subjects covered, see https://www.oxfordbibliographies.com/page/163.

15 https://heinonline.org/ (subscription database).

16 https://www.un.org/law/avl/.

CHAPTER 3

FOREIGN AND COMPARATIVE LAW

3.1 INTRODUCTION

The focus of this *Nutshell* is researching international law. Though international law is distinct from foreign and comparative law, I recognize that those doing international legal research often end up doing some foreign legal research as well. While research in comparative law used to be the province of academic writers, there is a greater interest in comparing laws and procedures than ever before. Therefore, it makes sense to cover it in this book as well, and I will address researching foreign and comparative law in this chapter. The field of foreign law is a vast one, so be forewarned that I will not go into great detail for any specific country. My goal will be to provide some basic strategies for locating and researching the domestic law of another country—also known as foreign law—with a bit of comparative law research advice in the section that follows.

For the purposes of this chapter, "foreign law" is the national (also referred to as domestic or internal) law of any country, other than the U.S. (Assuming that you are a researcher in the U.S.; if you are from another country, substitute its name). Comparative law is "the study of the similarities and differences between the laws of two or more countries, or between two or more legal systems. Comparative law is not itself a system of law or a body of rules, but rather a method or approach to legal inquiry."[1]

While research methods will vary depending on the country you are researching, when beginning to research a legal system, it's a good idea to get a basic understanding of the structure of that legal system. There are several ways to do this. First, determine if the country in question is a civil law system based upon codes that draw upon a Roman law heritage; a common law system (such as the U.S.) that springs from English tradition; or a mixed system. Some legal systems are also influenced by religious law or by custom. A quick way to determine the type of system for the country in question is to consult the free website JuriGlobe-World Legal Systems.[2] For more information on legal systems generally, see H. Patrick Glen, *Legal Traditions of the World* (5th ed. 2014).

---

1 Robert C. Berring et al., *How to Find the Law* 565 (12th ed. 2005).

2 https://www.juriglobe.ca/eng/.

Next, look for a source that explains the legal system of the country that you are researching. This is especially important if you do not have much background in the national system that you are approaching. Luckily there are some quite reliable sources for getting rich background information. Perhaps the most widely used and respected source is Foreign Law Guide.[3] This source will give you background on a given country, its legal system, its legal publications and, best of all, English-language sources and translations of materials, if available. An expert in the country you are researching could probably find mistakes in the description—which is no surprise since this set covers so much ground—but it is generally reliable and widely used. You should also see if a specific overview or a research guide is available for your country since these sources usually provide outlines of legal structures. Some ideas on how to find these resources will be covered later in this chapter.

3.2 CIVIL LAW VERSUS COMMON LAW

Before jumping into foreign legal research, you should understand some fundamentals of civil and common law. Civil law refers to a legal tradition based on Roman law and codified in the *Corpus Juris Civilis* of Justinian. This tradition, which initially developed in Continental Europe, eventually developed into codified Roman law and uncodified Roman law. A key feature of civil law is its system

---

[3] https://referenceworks.brill.com/display/db/flg (subscription database).

and structure, which often relies on declarations of broad, general principles.

The common law legal tradition evolved in England, beginning in the 11th century. Disputes that have been adjudicated comprise the set of principles that courts, usually courts of appeal, produce as judgments. Common law is the foundation of private law for England, Wales, Ireland, and forty-nine U.S. states, as well as most countries that inherited the legal system as colonies of the British Empire.

Below are some basic comparisons between the two systems. These are quite simplistic, but they do represent some fundamental differences.

CIVIL LAW JURISDICTIONS	**COMMON LAW JURISDICTIONS**
Rely primarily on legislation to develop and enact laws.	Rely primarily on court decisions to interpret legislation as well as develop law.
Historical Concept: A *single,* complete, coherent, and logical system to govern *all* legal relationships was possible to develop and follow.	Historical Concept: Legislation (by the ruling authority) was considered as a suspension of the "common law" that governed the everyday affairs of men; thus, people were suspicious of how legislation was to be applied.

CIVIL LAW JURISDICTIONS	COMMON LAW JURISDICTIONS
Favor predictability and stability but are generally very inflexible because they can be changed only by legislative action.	Favor flexibility, although predictability comes from the principle of *stare decisis* (do not disturb a settled point).
Civil law attorneys tend to interpret the law expansively to add the flexibility necessary to apply the legislation to new situations when they arise. However, the current trend in some civil law jurisdictions is for lawyers to keep informed about (and often use) prior judicial decisions in new cases.	While common law attorneys tend to interpret legislation narrowly, common law *courts* tend to interpret legislation more broadly than civil law courts, and this provides the flexibility to address new situations without new legislative action.
Trial judges have the responsibility to "find the truth." Thus, judges (the court) often identify the legal issue(s), investigate the facts, select and question the witnesses, and assume the procedural initiative.	Rely on the "adversary system"; thus, the court is "passive." The court solves only those issues that are put before it; the attorneys identify and frame the issues and then advocate for their respective sides. "Truth" is ultimately found by the court, with help from the jury, through the passive decision-making that separates persuasive

CIVIL LAW JURISDICTIONS	COMMON LAW JURISDICTIONS
	arguments and evidence from unpersuasive ones.
Rely primarily on deductive reasoning.	Rely on a combination of inductive, deductive, and analogical reasoning.

In a civil law system, primary sources include constitutions, statutes/codes, and regulations. Secondary sources include court decisions (jurisprudence) and scholarly commentary. In a common law system, primary sources include all of the above plus judicial decisions. The commentary of scholars is considered a secondary source. The rule of thumb is that in civil law countries, the code is paramount, and decisions of the court are just interpretations of the code. In common law countries, judicial decisions are statements of the law itself. Of course, this is an extreme simplification, but it is a basis from which to build. Most commentators feel that the two systems are moving closer to one another as time passes. For more information on civil and common law, see John G. Apple & Robert P. Deyling, *A Primer on the Civil-Law System* (1995).[4]

3.3 TYPES OF SOURCES

Constitutions are widely available both in the original language and in English. Several websites are available to access these primary documents, see

[4] https://www.govinfo.gov/app/details/GOVPUB-JU13-PURL-LPS55055.

for example Constitute[5] and the Council of Europe CODICES database.[6] These are good sources, and they are free. Constitute is part of a larger project on comparing constitutions, and it allows you to compare constitutions by topic as well as search and download the text of constitutions. Two other widely available databases are by subscription: World Constitutions Illustrated (HeinOnline) and Oxford Constitutions of the World.[7] Because constitutions are so fundamental, specialized resources are being created. For example, the Global Gender Equality Constitutional Database is a collection of gender equality-related provisions in 194 constitutions from around the world.[8] See also Max Planck Encyclopedia of Comparative Constitutional Law, an online resource providing a global overview of constitutional law.[9] The Foreign Law Guide[10] and country-specific research guides also provide links to constitutions and other foundational documents as well as commentary and analysis on national constitutional law. Keep in mind that some countries may not have a written constitution but have a collection of foundational documents.

---

5 https://www.constituteproject.org/.

6 https://www.venice.coe.int/WebForms/pages/?p=01_CODICES_constitutions&lang=EN.

7 https://heinonline.org/ (subscription database) and https://oxcon.ouplaw.com/ (subscription database).

8 https://constitutions.unwomen.org/en.

9 Available on the Oxford Constitutional Law database, https://oxcon.ouplaw.com/.

10 https://referenceworks.brill.com/display/db/flg (subscription database).

Statutory law is prevalent in both kinds of legal systems and is published in several types of sources:

- Official or national gazettes (usually released daily by national governments, these may contain laws, notices, and other information).
- Session laws (laws published chronologically, in print or electronic form).
- Codified Laws (a subject arrangement of laws).
- Subject compilations, other than codes.

Court decisions are also available from a variety of sources:

- Official reporters (publications deemed as the primary and official source of case law).
- Commercial or unofficial sources (many websites would be considered unofficial, even a Court's site).
- Journals (used a great deal in some jurisdictions, like Germany and France).
- Topic-specific compilations.

3.4 DEVELOPING A RESEARCH STRATEGY

Once you understand the nature of the legal system in question, you should determine exactly what you need. Do you need a constitution, a specific statute, a case, or general information about a country's legal system? Do you have a citation to the law or to an article? What are the relevant dates? Do you need the complete text of the law, a summary, an

English translation, or a detailed explanation? Will an electronic version be sufficient, or do you need an official print source? Here are some tips to help answer these many questions:

- Use a secondary source to start your research. These sources describe the law or legal issue, provide commentary, and put the issue into context.
- Identify the sources of law for the country. Does the country publish codes, compilations of statutes, or reporters? A good source for gathering this information is Foreign Law Guide (noted above).
- Once you have identified the source, consult a library catalog or a database to determine if the item is available.

As noted above, using a research guide or an introductory source is a good place to begin researching the law or legal system of another country. Most of these kinds of tools will outline the structure of the legal system and the sources of law that are available. You can find research guides and introductions in journal articles or in chapters of a more general book.

I have already mentioned the granddaddy of all such sources: Foreign Law Guide. This source is one of the best to consult when researching foreign law. It contains information on nearly 190 jurisdictions, and each country section contains the following information: a brief history of the legal system (including references to other introductory sources);

an outline of the major publications (including major codifications, official gazettes, compilations or official codifications, session laws, court reports, and electronic resources); and a section of laws organized by subject headings. While this source does not cover every country or every law within a country, it does contain a lot of information and is always worth consulting.

While there is no other source that covers as many countries as the Foreign Law Guide, there are a few other basic sources to consult at the start of any research project. You might also check the *Guide to International Legal Research* (2002–),[11] "Guide to Law Online: Nations of the World" from the Law Library of Congress,[12] Yale Law Library's "Country by Country Guide to Foreign Legal Research,"[13] and GlobaLex.[14] As ever, consult a librarian about what sources are available in your library.

Legal researchers are fortunate that the web is such a useful vehicle for accessing country-specific legal research guides. The following web search (using your favorite search engine) is effective for locating such guides: [name of country] legal research guide or [topic] legal research guide.

While you can access many research guides and a lot of information on the web, some introductions to

---

[11] Also available on Lexis.

[12] https://guides.loc.gov/nations-world.

[13] https://library.law.yale.edu/research-guides/country-country-guide-foreign-legal-research.

[14] https://www.nyulawglobal.org/globalex. See the comparative law and the foreign law tabs.

the law of a country are in print sources. For example, Peter Maggs et al., *Law and Legal System of the Russian Federation* (7th ed. 2020), Daniel C.K. Chow et al., *The Legal System of the People's Republic of China in a Nutshell* (4th ed. 2023), and *Introduction to Turkish Law* (Tŭgrul Ansay & Don Wallace, Jr., eds., 7th ed. 2020).

When looking for laws or information on a specific legal system consider sources that focus on the geographic region, a topic, or include the words like "global" or "world" in the title. These kinds of sources may also contain sections or chapters on individual countries. For example, *Handbook on Legal Cultures: A Selection of the World's Legal Cultures* (Sören Koch & Marius Mikkel Kjølstad, eds., 2023) or *The Oxford Handbook of Constitutional Law in Asia* (David S. Law, Holning Lau & Alex Schwartz, eds., 2023).

Foreign jurisdictions may use unfamiliar abbreviations for legal sources. Many of the sources for deciphering abbreviations are listed in Chapter 2 of this *Nutshell*. However, some abbreviations can be located in the source itself, or you may need a guide that focuses on a single jurisdiction, like, Francisco Avalos, *Avalos Legal Glossary/Dictionary Translator and Other Related Fields of Study: English/Spanish Spanish/English* (2018). A very handy guide is the *International Citator and Research Guide: The Greenbook* (2018–). This tool provides information on available legal sources and how to abbreviate and cite them.

3.5 LOOKING FOR FOREIGN LAW

There are generally two approaches to looking for foreign law—by subject or by jurisdiction. If you are looking for a specific piece of legislation, the tools mentioned above are very useful. Foreign Law Guide is particularly useful for this purpose because it contains a listing of selected laws arranged by subject for each country. Country-specific research guides may not provide guidance for all laws, but they will provide information on compilations of laws or specific codes. Be sure to look for subject compilations; for example, laws on investment are contained in a set called *Investment Laws of the World* (1972–). As mentioned above, also consider sources from the region where the country is located, such as *Company Law in Europe* (1992–).

Another rather extensive source is *International Encyclopaedia of Laws*[15] (dates vary). Arranged by topic (civil procedure, contracts, environmental law, family and succession, social security, etc.), it covers many jurisdictions and provides narrative information with citations to relevant laws. Each topic covers different countries, so don't assume all topics have the same jurisdictional coverage. Be sure to note the date the chapter was last updated since some content may be dated. This set also includes some basic information about the country's legal system. Take note of two other useful encyclopedias: *Elgar Encyclopedia of Comparative Law* (Jan M. Smits et al., eds., 2023–) and *Encyclopedia of Private*

[15] https://www.kluwerlawonline.com/index.php (subscription database).

International Law (Jürgen Basedow et al., eds., 2017–).[16] Both contain subject entries and country chapters. The country chapters provide good outlines on the law and legal system for each jurisdiction covered.

Be on the lookout for subject compilations, digests, and websites that cover your topic. Often, these sources use words like "world" or "international" in the title. Subject compilations such as *Digest of Commercial Laws of the World* (1998–),[17] *Data Protection Laws of the World* (1988–), *International Securities Regulation* (2012–) and RefWorld[18] can be of great help. You will note that they tend to treat topics that generate cross border transactions and business. Foreign Law Guide provides a good listing of subject compilations under the secondary sources noted for each subject.

Another very good resource for identifying relevant secondary sources by country or subjects is *Multinational Sources Compared: A Subject and Jurisdiction Index* (2021).[19] The aim is to provide researchers with information on sources, both print and electronic, that cover multiple jurisdictions on

---

16 Both encyclopedias are available at https://www.elgaronline.com (subscription databases).

17 Available on Westlaw.

18 Produced by the UN High Commissioner for Refugees, it provides law and jurisprudence related to refugees, migrants, etc., https://www.refworld.org/.

19 Available HeinOnline, https://heinonline.org/ (subscription database).

specific subjects. The sources listed may provide full-text legislation, commentary, or citations to law.

Searching the library catalogs of different law libraries may also be useful for identifying relevant sources by country or topic. It's important to understand that while you cannot access the sources listed using these two tools, you can identify needed materials and perhaps access them from a library or a database.

While official gazettes (official journals) are not the most user-friendly tools to use, they are often the first place where laws are officially published. Many gazettes are only available in print, some are available on government websites[20] and commercial databases, and others are available through Foreign Legal Gazettes database (Law Library of Congress)[21] which contains records for approximately from many national and subnational jurisdictions. In some cases, however, the gazettes are only available in print at the Law Library of Congress or another library.

Secondary legislation, regulations, and administrative decisions are often sought-after and can be even more elusive than statutory law and case law. Start by using the sources mentioned in the

[20] For example, Légifrance, https://www.legifrance.gouv.fr/.

[21] https://loc.maps.arcgis.com/apps/dashboards/72089675f5e845f99d8e6c12e892b96a#p1=Complete. For more information on how to use this collection, see Stephen Mayeaux, "Bite-Sized Legal Research Tutorial: Foreign Legal Gazettes Guide," https://blogs.loc.gov/law/2024/07/bite-sized-legal-research-tutorial-foreign-legal-gazettes-guide/.

above sections. Secondary sources may be another way to track down relevant sources. If a country publishes an official gazette (as most civil law systems do), you have a better chance of locating regulations, notices, circulars, etc. Some countries include secondary (or subsidiary) legislation with the relevant statutory law; for example, see Singapore Statutes Online.[22] Other jurisdictions make the rules and regulations available from the same website; see legislation.gov.uk for access to secondary legislation for the UK, Scotland, Wales and Northern Ireland.

A project worth mentioning is the Free Access to Law Movement (FALM),[23] an association of more than 60 organizations from around the world who provide free access to legal information. These associations include World Legal Information Institute (WorldLII),[24] African Legal Information Institute (AfricanLII),[25] the Australasian Legal Information Institute (AustLII),[26] and many more. Many of these databases include case law, legislation, treaties, law reform reports, law journals, and other materials. With any freely available websites, the researcher should always try to discern if the site is up-to-date.

Case law is much more challenging to locate in both the vernacular and in translation. Keep in mind that in civil law countries, case law is not a source of

---

22 https://sso.agc.gov.sg/.

23 http://www.falm.info/.

24 http://www.worldlii.org/.

25 https://africanlii.org/.

26 http://www.austlii.edu.au/.

primary law, and there may not be any official publication of decisions. Access to cases will vary from country to country, depending on many factors. In some countries, only the country's highest court will publicly issue its decisions. Some databases, like AustLII, include court decisions from various national courts.

Web databases are being developed that contain case law from various jurisdictions based on a topic or even by region. For example, the Human Trafficking Knowledge Portal[27] hosts a case law database containing national court decisions related to human trafficking crimes. There's also the Global Health and Human Rights Database,[28] a collection of national cases from around the world relating to health and human rights issues (health care and services, mental health, hospitals, and the like). Another kind of collection is Juricaf,[29] a compilation of supreme court decisions from 48 francophone countries (available only in French, of course).

There really is no single, complete source for all case law (print or electronic), even for a specific jurisdiction (with some exceptions). To locate reporters, both official and unofficial, check the sections on "Court Reports" in Foreign Law Guide. This section will tell you whether the country issues official reports or if you must look in other sources, such as periodicals. In many countries, legal

---

27 https://sherloc.unodc.org/cld/en/st/home.html.

28 https://www.globalhealthrights.org/.

29 https://juricaf.org/.

periodicals act as unofficial sources for court decisions, e.g., *Neue Juristische Wochenschrift* (NJW) (1947–) [Germany]. Even articles in journal literature can be of assistance when searching for domestic cases. For example, *The Korean Journal of International and Comparative Law* (2013–)[30] has a regular section that outlines major decisions from Korean courts. The *International Journal of Refugee Law* (1989–) provides case law summaries in each issue. Other kinds of case law compilations exist, such as *Law Reports of the Commonwealth* (1994–), which covers key cases from the United Kingdom and Commonwealth countries.

If you need to decipher a case citation, one of the best sources to use is *Noble's Revised International Guide to the Law Reports* (2002) or the Cardiff Index to Legal Abbreviations.[31] Both of these sources are a bit dated. Be sure to consult country research guides (noted above) for further assistance.

Chapter 6 of this *Nutshell* focuses on researching international case law and includes some topical sources that contain domestic cases. See also Appendix B for selected websites and databases for foreign law.

3.6 TRANSLATED MATERIAL

Most U.S. lawyers and law students want foreign laws to appear in English, even if they have the requisite language abilities. There are many sources

---

30 Available electronically from Brill.

31 https://www.legalabbrevs.cardiff.ac.uk/.

that have English language translations, some available by country, by region, or by topic. Be aware of the limitations of translations:

- Translations, even if done under the auspices of a government agency, are not necessarily official or authoritative. The only exceptions are jurisdictions where English is one of the official languages. For example, Canada publishes all laws in both English and French. The goal is to locate a reliable translation.

- Translations can be inaccurate. Many legal terms and phrases do not mean the same thing in every language or every legal system. Think of the problems of jargon and word usage encountered by students in law school. Add in a different language and perhaps a different legal structure, and the problem becomes apparent. Be sure the translation was done by someone with knowledge of the country's legal system.

- Translations may not include the most current revisions of the law.

- Translations take time and new laws or amendments may not be available as soon as you need them.

- Some topics have more translations than other topics; areas such as business, trade, taxation, and commercial law tend to have more English-language sources than areas dealing with family law or social issues.

Translations can be found in a variety of sources, such as books, journals, loose-leaf sets, subscription databases, and websites. As mentioned above, there are many English-language compilations, especially in the areas of taxation, trade, commercial, and business law. Other areas of law may not have readily available English translations.

Another thing to consider is the date of the translation. Be sure to read the translated version carefully because some compilations may contain only an abstract of the law or an explanation and not the full text of the law.

Loose-leaf services (sources that are frequently updated) and journals can be fruitful sources for English translations. The Foreign Law Guide is a very good source for translations. Research guides can also provide access or information on translations. Many loose-leaf services are transforming into web databases (by subscription) or are available in print and online.

There are also some good websites for accessing reliable translations by subject. Many of these websites are created by international organizations. Some of these include WIPO Lex[32] or the ILO's NATLEX database.[33] For more such collections, see

---

[32] Produced by the World Intellectual Property Organization, it contains national laws related to intellectual property, https://www.wipo.int/en/web/wipolex.

[33] Produced by the International Labor Organization, it provides access to national law related to labor, social security and related issues, https://natlex.ilo.org/dyn/natlex2/r/natlex/fe/home.

Jennifer Allison, "Foreign Law—Subject Law Collections on the Web."[34]

Looking for case law from other jurisdictions in English is a common research problem. There are more sources for translated cases available on the web, but they tend to be selective in the cases translated and the topics covered. Some good representative examples include ESCR-Net Caselaw Database[35] and the Codices database.[36]

A few sources for translated cases include *International Law Reports* (1919–),[37] *International Labour Law Reports* (1978–), *e-Bulletin on Constitutional Case-Law* (1993–),[38] and the *East European Case Reporter of Constitutional Law* (1994–). Some compilations focus on a single jurisdiction: prominent sets include *Decisions of the Korean Constitutional Court* (2000–),[39] or *Selected Judgments of the Supreme Court of Israel* (1962–). Oxford Reports on International Law[40] contains

---

34 https://www.nyulawglobal.org/globalex/foreign_collections1.html.

35 Legal Decisions regarding economic, social, and cultural rights, https://www.escr-net.org/caselaw.

36 Contains constitutional case law, produced by the Council of Europe's Venice Commission, https://codices.coe.int/codices/documents/welcome.

37 Available on vLex, https://vlex.com/ (subscription database).

38 Available on Codices Database, https://www.venice.coe.int/WebForms/pages/?p=02_02_Bulletins.

39 Also available on the Court's website, https://english.ccourt.go.kr/site/eng/main.do and https://library.ccourt.go.kr/en/#/about/pub/case.

40 https://opil.ouplaw.com/home/oril (subscription database).

English translations of selected national cases dealing with a variety of international law topics, such as human rights, trade, treaties, etc.

Some cases are translated and freely available on the web and may be located by consulting the research guides mentioned above. Some examples of the kinds of sites available include WorldLII Courts & Case-Law[41] and RefWorld.[42] WorldLII is a directory of websites organized by country, whereas RefWorld is a database containing cases related to refugee law from 60 national jurisdictions. Some sites provide access to selected decisions in English. For example, the Institute for Transnational Law at the University of Texas at Austin Law School provides translated decisions for France, Germany, Israel, and Austria.[43]

Some websites provide national laws or codes in English. Each of these sites varies as to the number of translations provided and the focus of material chosen. FinLex contains many English translations of Finnish acts and decrees.[44] Other good examples include Japanese Law Translation and Germans Laws on the Internet.[45] To locate more of these sites,

---

[41] http://www.worldlii.org/catalog/2172.html.

[42] https://www.refworld.org/collections/case-law.

[43] https://law.utexas.edu/transnational/foreign-law-translations/.

[44] https://www.finlex.fi/en/.

[45] https://www.japaneselawtranslation.go.jp/ and https://www.gesetze-im-internet.de/Teilliste_translations.html.

consult research guides, like Foreign Law Guide, a country research guide, or WorldLII.[46]

As business becomes increasingly global in nature, many more databases will emerge that provide access to foreign law in English. In fact, there are several subscription services available, such as CIS Legislation (English and Russian legislation from the Commonwealth of Independent States), Global Regulation (covers many jurisdictions), and China LawInfo.[47] Topic specific databases, usually available only by subscription, are good places to check for English translations. As noted above, these databases tend to focus on commercial, investment, and related areas of law. Databases include IBFD Tax Research Platform, Kluwer Arbitration, and Kluwer IP.[48]

Many researchers turn to web-based translators when confronted with a page in an unfamiliar language.[49] These tools can be used to help give an idea of the topic of the web document or for translating specific terms or phrases. While machine translations have improved over the years, use

---

[46] http://www.worldlii.org/countries.html.

[47] See Appendix B for databases.

[48] See Appendix A for databases.

[49] There are many such translators: DeepL (https://www.deepl.com/ko/translator), BabelFish (https://www.babelfish.com/), Bing Translator (https://www.bing.com/translator), and Google Translate (https://translate.google.com/). For more information on these translators, see the University of Iowa Law Library's research guide, "Legal Interpreting and Translating: Online Resources," http://libguides.law.uiowa.edu/c.php?g=103196&p=669077.

caution because they are not always accurate. Some of the generative AI (GenAI) tools may also be useful for translations legal documents.[50] These tools may not be any more reliable than Google Translate or Bing. For more information on GenAI tools, see Chapter 14 of this *Nutshell*.

Of course, when no translation exists or you need help with a single word or phrase, bilingual or multilingual dictionaries are useful tools. Most of these dictionaries related to law are not readily available on the web, but a few are available on Lexis. Some common dictionaries include *West's Law and Commercial Dictionary in Five Languages: Definitions of the Legal and Commercial Terms and Phrases of American, English and Civil Law Jurisdictions* (1985) and *Dahl's French-English Law Dictionary* (2007) and *Dahl's Spanish-English Law Dictionary* (2015). Like online translators, dictionaries do not provide any context for terms. However, unlike online translators, they are geared for legal communications. Once again, check with your librarian concerning which dictionaries are available to you.

3.7 COMPARATIVE LAW

As mentioned above, comparative law is a form of study and not a body of law. Comparative law books and materials present information in several different ways. Some focus on comparing legal

---

[50] Amanda Lee, May 23, 2024, "The Best AI Translators for Legal Translations in 2024," https://beringlab.com/2024/05/23/the-best-ai-translators-for-legal-translations-in-2024/.

families or traditions (civil law versus common law, ancient law, etc.). Some books compare specific countries (German law as compared to French law). Others focus on comparing topics within laws and within countries (constitutional law in Germany and the U.S.). And some sources do all of the above.

The comparative law researcher should have a clear understanding of how government institutions and legal systems function. To understand how they function, you need to have an awareness of the legal, economic, and social context.

Researching comparative law usually means looking for foreign law and any related commentary. Use the tools outlined above on locating foreign law and information about foreign legal systems. Some handy sources to start with are available in both print and electronic form. See the *Oxford Handbook of Comparative Law* (Mathias Reimann & Reinhard Zimmermann, eds., 2nd ed. 2019), *The Cambridge Handbook of Comparative Law* (Mathias Siems & Po Jen Yap., eds., 2024), *Elgar Encyclopedia of Comparative Law* (Jan M. Smits, ed., 2023—),[51] and Mary Ann Glendon, *Comparative Legal Traditions in a Nutshell* (4th ed. 2015).[52] There are many books on comparative law and method. Check your library's catalog.

---

51 Available electronically at https://www.elgaronline.com (subscription database).

52 Available electronically on West Academic (subscription database).

Some research guides also address comparative law generally or on a specific comparative law topic. The GlobaLex website has a section on comparative law research and includes guides on comparative law generally, comparative civil procedure, and comparative criminal procedure.[53] Other more general guides on this site are also useful, such as Foreign Law: Subject Law Collections on the Web.[54]

The Law Library of Congress produces legal research reports that provide commentary, citations to relevant laws, and recommended sources on a variety of issues.[55] Some of these reports are comparative in nature—for example, "Carbon Neutrality Legislation Around the World" or "Regulation of Artificial Intelligence Around the World." Some reports focus on a particular jurisdiction as well, such as "South Korea: Public Prosecution Reform."[56]

For those of you who are familiar with *American Law Reports* (ALR), you may want to use *ALR International: Annotations and Cases* (2010–)[57] for your comparative law research. It is just like other ALRs, but it analyzes relevant U.S. and foreign cases from English and non-English speaking countries on specific international legal issues (service abroad,

---

[53] https://www.nyulawglobal.org/globalex/index.html.

[54] https://www.nyulawglobal.org/globalex/Foreign_Collections1.html.

[55] https://www.loc.gov/collections/publications-of-the-law-library-of-congress/about-this-collection/.

[56] https://www.loc.gov/item/2023555904/.

[57] Also available on Westlaw.

patent infringement, sovereign debt, and much more).

Searching the web for comparative law surveys or databases can be quite fruitful. Law firms and international organizations post many useful reports and documents. For example, the World Bank has a very good background paper on mapping data governance legal frameworks around the world.[58]

In the areas of business and taxation, there are some good subscription sources aimed at legal practitioners. For taxation, the International Bureau of Fiscal Documentation (IBFD) is a comprehensive tax platform through which you can create detailed country comparison charts. A series called Panoramic (formerly *Getting the Deal Through*) covers 150 jurisdictions and 120 practice areas (such as, competition, white collar crime, banking and finance, etc.) and these annual reviews are written by lawyers who work in the particular subject area and jurisdiction. These are available on Bloomberg Law, but the stand-alone database allows you to create useful comparison charts.[59] Westlaw also provides access to "Practical Law" and it contains a section called "Global Content." From here, you can view "global guides" on various topics, such as "investing in" and get overviews of the legal climate for

---

[58] "Mapping Data Governance Legal Frameworks Around the World: Findings from the Global Data Regulation Diagnostic," https://openknowledge.worldbank.org/entities/publication/8a6cb591-4548-5786-b108-5f9cd32edc8c.

[59] https://www.lexology.com/panoramic (subscription database) and Bloomberg Law (subscription database).

investing (including references to relevant laws) for several countries.[60] There is also a "Country Q & A Comparison Tool" which allows you to compare subjects for multiple jurisdictions. Lexis has a set of resources called "Practical Guidance" and these are similar to Practical Law on Westlaw. Also included are Multilaw Global Guides and they cover a variety of topics and jurisdictions, for example, "Multilaw Global Guide: How to Hire and Fire (Argentina)."[61]

Another handy comparative tool is the International Comparative Legal Guides (ICLG).[62] These guides cover 58 practice areas (copyright, family law, enforcement of foreign judgments, etc.) and 112 jurisdictions. Some content is available for free on the ICLG website, and you can also purchase the guides as a book or a PDF chapter. These are written by lawyers in the specific jurisdictions and provide references to relevant laws and procedures.

Some subscription databases provide access to law across jurisdictions and allow comparative law searching, such as vLex, and Global Regulation.[63] The vLex database also allows the researcher to translate search terms into different languages.

There is a whole collection of comparative law journals and lots of articles in other journals on comparative law issues. Some examples include the

---

[60] Available on Westlaw.

[61] Available on Lexis.

[62] https://iclg.com.

[63] These are all subscription databases, see Appendix A for websites.

American Journal of Comparative Law (1952–), the *Journal of Comparative Law in Africa* (2014–), and the *Global Journal of Comparative Law* (2012–). See also the open access journals—for example, the *German Law Journal* reporting on German and European legal developments.[64] For more information on locating journal articles, please see Chapter 10 of this *Nutshell*.

3.8 HARD TO FIND MATERIALS

While a good deal of foreign and comparative law is available online or in print, there are still pockets of hard to locate legal materials.

- Administrative regulations and decisions (especially in English).
- Forms.
- State and local law.
- Dockets, briefs and court documents.[65]
- Older or superceded laws.

---

64 https://germanlawjournal.com/.

65 For some help in this area, see UCLA Law Library, "Dockets and Court Documents by Country," https://libguides.law.ucla.edu/internationaldockets.

CHAPTER 4

TREATIES AND INTERNATIONAL AGREEMENTS

4.1 INTRODUCTION

Treaties are basically written agreements between States that are governed by international law. Locating the text of a treaty, or researching information about a particular treaty, is one of the most common types of international legal research.

While many treaties are readily available on the web, some agreements may only be available in print sources. This is especially true when looking for an older or more obscure agreement between two countries. Note that not all countries make treaties and agreements available on government websites.

4.2 SOME BASICS

Treaties can be referred to by several different names: international conventions, international agreements, covenants, final acts, charters, protocols, pacts, accords, or constitutions for international organizations. Usually, these different names have no legal significance in international law. Treaties may be bilateral (between two parties) or multilateral (among several parties) and are usually only binding on the parties to the agreement. An agreement "enters into force" when the terms for entry into force specified in the agreement are met. Bilateral treaties usually enter into force when both parties agree to be bound as of a certain date.

Much of the structure and rules about treaty making are set forth in the Vienna Convention on the Law of Treaties.[1] This treaty sets out basic definitions, identifies an authentic text, provides information on reservations, and the like. This treaty is so important that some of the articles have become custom rules of international law (customary international law is covered in Chapter 5 of this

---

[1] 1155 U.N.T.S. 331 (May 23, 1969), https://treaties.un.org/doc/Publication/UNTS/Volume%201155/volume-1155-I-18232-English.pdf.

Nutshell). A detailed examination of seminal treaties is available in *The Vienna Convention on the Law of Treaties: A Commentary* (2011).

For more basic information on treaties, see Thomas Buergenthal & Sean Murphy, *Public International Law in a Nutshell* (6th ed. 2019), *The Oxford Guide to Treaties* (Duncan Hollis, ed., 2nd ed. 2020), or Robert Kolb, *The Law of Treaties: An Introduction* (2nd ed. 2023). For basic definitions of treaty terminology, see the United Nations, *Treaty Handbook* (rev. ed. 2013).[2]

4.3 GETTING STARTED

As a researcher, you usually face the following treaty research problems:

- Locating the text of the treaty or agreement, including any updates.
- Obtaining status and ratification information, effective dates, and a list of the parties.
- Finding the text of any reservations and declarations.
- Determining if national implementing legislation is needed and/or available.
- Looking at the intent and interpretation of the treaty through background documents,

---

2 https://treaties.un.org/pages/Resource.aspx?path=Publication/TH/Page1_en.xml.

negotiations, legislative history, or court decisions.

When you have the name of a treaty and need the text, your first instinct is probably to search the web using Google. While this may bring up many sites for obtaining the text of the agreement, it is not always the best way to begin treaty research. Some treaties go by a popular name or an acronym that may not be useful in a Google search. For example, a search on Google will retrieve over four million hits for "Hague conventions." While you will learn that there are many Hague conventions, you may not be able to determine which one is the relevant document. If you know something about the topic of the treaty, adding more keywords to your search will yield more worthwhile results. A more targeted research tool is the Flare Index to Treaties, a searchable database of more than 2,000 multilateral treaties concluded from the 1600s to present.[3] This database allows searching with keywords as well as with year and place concluded. Entries provide links to the text of the treaty and "published in" information, which is useful for getting citations to print publications, like U.N.T.S. Like many other web resources, the Flare Index does not cover every available agreement, it covers the "most significant treaties, conventions and agreements."[4]

---

[3] https://ials.sas.ac.uk/digital/ials-digital-resources/flare-index-treaties.

[4] See the homepage of the Flare Index to Treaties.

Keep in mind that the research guides mentioned in other chapters of this *Nutshell* may also cover treaties and agreements.

4.4 U.S. TREATIES AND AGREEMENTS

A. BACKGROUND INFORMATION

Before delving into treaties too deeply, a few words about U.S. treaties and agreements are in order. Domestically, treaties to which the U.S. is a party are equivalent in status to Federal legislation, forming part of what the Constitution calls 'the supreme Law of the Land.'[5] Yet, the word "treaty" does not have the same meaning in the U.S. as it does under international law.[6] The Vienna Convention on the Law of Treaties defines a treaty "as an international agreement concluded between States in written form and governed by international law, whether embodied in a single instrument or in two or more related instruments and whatever its particular designation."[7] Under U.S. law, however, there is a distinction between the terms *treaty* and *executive agreement*. In the U.S., the word "treaty" is reserved

---

5 U.S. Constitution art. VI, § 2, cl. 2, https://constitution.congress.gov/browse/article-6/clause-2/.

6 *Treaties and Other International Agreements: The Role of the United States Senate: A Study*, prepared for the Committee on Foreign Relations, United States Senate, S. Print 106–71, at 1 (2001), available at https://www.govinfo.gov/content/pkg/CPRT-106SPRT66922/pdf/CPRT-106SPRT66922.pdf.

7 Vienna Convention on the Law of Treaties, 1155 U.N.T.S. 311 (May 23, 1969), art. 2, s 1(a), available at https://treaties.un.org/doc/Publication/UNTS/Volume%201155/volume-1155-I-18232-English.pdf.

for an agreement that is made 'by and with the Advice and Consent of the Senate.[8] International agreements not submitted to the Senate are known as 'executive agreements' in the U.S.[9] Regardless of whether an international agreement is called a convention, agreement, protocol, accord, etc.; if it is submitted to the Senate for advice and consent, it is considered a treaty under U.S. law.

A common misconception is that all U.S. treaties and agreements are freely available on the web. While there are collections of instruments, there is no one comprehensive collection for them all, especially not for free.

1. Full-Text Sources

Until 1950, U.S. treaties appeared regularly after proclamation in *Statutes at Large* (1789–). Pre-1950 treaties can also be found in *Treaties and Other International Agreements of the United States of America, 1776–1949* (1968–1976).[10] This 13-volume set is commonly cited by the compilers' name, Bevans. In 1950, *United States Treaties and Other International Agreements* (cited as U.S.T.) (1950–1984) became the official source for all U.S. treaties and agreements. Several volumes were published annually, each with a non-cumulative subject and country index.

---

[8] U.S. Constitution art. VI, § 2, cl. 2, https://constitution.congress.gov/browse/article-6/clause-2/, supra note 4.

[9] *Treaties and Other International Agreements: The Role of the United States Senate: A Study*, supra note 6.

[10] https://www.loc.gov/law/help/us-treaties/bevans.php.

U.S. treaties first appeared in slip form in *Treaties and Other International Acts Series* (cited as T.I.A.S.) (1946–2016),[11] a set of individually paginated pamphlets, consecutively numbered. However, the Government Printing Office (GPO) no longer publishes the TIAS or UST in print. Since 2002, treaties and non-treaty acts have a new numbering system. The number can be derived from the entry-into-force date of the agreement. For example, a document with the number "02–306" came into force on March 6, 2002.

After ratification, selected treaties (once they are cleared for publication by the Senate) are published in the *Senate Treaty Document Series* (1981–) (formerly the *Senate Executive Document Series*).[12] Pursuant to 1 U.S.C. § 112a,[13] the Secretary of State is required to publish agreements on the State Department's website no later than 180 days after the date on which the treaty or agreement enters into force. This collection begins with the year 1981.[14]

2. Treaty Indexes

There are several indexes and guides that provide citations to treaties and agreements where the U.S. is a party. The most common is *Treaties in Force*

---

[11] https://www.state.gov/tias/.

[12] Senate Treaty Documents are available on the web from the 81st Congress (1949–1950) to present, https://www.congress.gov/treaties.

[13] https://www.law.cornell.edu/uscode/text/1/112a. For more information on this code section, see https://2009-2017.state.gov/s/l/treaty/tias/pubtias/index.htm.

[14] https://www.state.gov/tias/.

(TIF),[15] published by the U.S. Department of State. This publication, supplemented annually, lists and provides basic information for almost all U.S. treaties and agreements in force. It is arranged by country and subject; includes both bilateral and multilateral treaties; and it provides citations to U.S.T. and T.I.A.S. (if they are available). The primary use of TIF is verification of the existence of a treaty. At the time of publishing this *Nutshell*, the most recent version of TIF available is 2020, and it is split into bilateral and multilateral. TIF is also available on Lexis and Westlaw. Where possible, TIF on Lexis and Westlaw links to the text of the treaty. TIF is also available on HeinOnline from 1929 to present.

Because TIF is not always satisfactory for treaty research, there are some other tools available. *A Guide to the United States Treaties in Force* (I. Kavass and A. Sprudzs, eds., 1982–) is an annual publication and should be used in conjunction with TIF. This guide contains a combined subject index for both bilateral and multilateral treaties, as well as a numerical and a country index. This guide is also available on HeinOnline. It is supplemented by *Guide to the United States Treaties in Force: Current Treaty Action Supplement*.

Also published by Hein is the *United States Treaty Index* (I. Kavass, ed., 1991–). This is one of the most comprehensive sources for U.S. treaty information. There are subject, chronological, and country indexes. This set is supplemented by *Current Treaty*

---

[15] https://www.state.gov/treaties-in-force/.

Index, (I. Kavass and A. Sprudzs, eds., 1982–), a loose-leaf index listing current treaties that is published in slip form in T.I.A.S. as well as those treaties without T.I.A.S. numbers. The treaties are available on *Hein's United States Treaties and Other International Agreements* and on HeinOnline.

Another good treaty tool is Congress.Gov, Treaty Documents. This web collection contains all treaties submitted to the Senate since the 81st Congress (1949–1950). Search by Congress, treaty document number, word/phrase, or by type of treaty.[16]

Many of these same tools can be used to obtain status and ratification information. For example, TIF is a good source for determining which treaties and agreements are in force for the U.S.

3. Other Full-Text Sources

Because the official publication of U.S. treaties and agreements has traditionally been slow, other sources have filled the gap. Treaties are available on Lexis, Westlaw, and HeinOnline.[17] Each of these databases provides access to many of the treaties and agreements, but none of these services is complete on its own.

As noted above, most treaties and agreements are freely available on the web. Other federal government agencies provide access to agreements, such as the International Trade Administration's

---

[16] https://www.congress.gov/treaties.

[17] See the "U.S. Treaties and Agreements Library" (subscription database).

Trade and Related Agreements Database (TARA),[18] the U.S. Trade Representative's online collection of trade agreements and bilateral investment treaties,[19] and the online collection of U.S. income tax treaties from the IRS website.[20]

Legal scholars have written about the "slow death" of the U.S. treaty process.[21] The number of treaties concluded in each administration has declined. For example, during the Clinton administration, approximately 23 treaties were concluded each year. The Obama administration concluded approximately 5 treaties per year.[22] Declining numbers have also impacted executive agreements.[23] This decline in treaties and agreements has led to an increase in nonbinding international agreements. The problem is "nonbinding agreements have had no central repository and have not been subject to any rules about transparency or publication."[24] If such an

---

[18] https://www.trade.gov/all-trade-agreements.

[19] https://ustr.gov/trade-agreements.

[20] https://www.irs.gov/businesses/international-businesses/united-states-income-tax-treaties-a-to-z.

[21] Oona A. Hathaway, Curtis A. Bradley & Jack L. Goldsmith, "The Failed Transparency Regime for Executive Agreements: An Empirical and Normative Analysis," 134 *Harv. L. Rev.* 629 (2020), https://harvardlawreview.org/print/vol-134/the-failed-transparency-regime-for-executive-agreements/.

[22] *Id.* at 632.

[23] Jeffrey S. Peake, "The Decline of Treaties? Obama, Trump, and the Politics of International Agreements" (April 6, 2018). Available at SSRN: https://ssrn.com/abstract=3153840 or http://dx.doi.org/10.2139/ssrn.3153840.

[24] Curtis Bradley, Jack Goldsmith & Oona Hathaway, "The Rise of Nonbinding International Agreements: An Empirical, Comparative, and Normative Analysis," 90 *Univ. Chicago L. Rev.*

agreement has been made publicly available, the researcher must rely on internet searches to locate the text of the agreements. These nonbinding agreements include bilateral and multilateral agreements.

When researching U.S. treaties and agreements, be aware of the National Defense Authorization Act for Fiscal Year 2023 (NDAA).[25] This law expands the Case-Zablocki Act, adding reporting and publication requirements to qualifying non-binding instruments.

4.5 BILATERAL AND MULTILATERAL TREATIES AND AGREEMENTS

A. BILATERAL TREATIES

Locating bilateral treaties where the U.S. is not a party can be more challenging. Many bilateral agreements are published in the *United Nations Treaty Series* (cited as U.N.T.S.). Nevertheless, you may still need to look at collections by country or topic.

1281, 1286 (2023), https://lawreview.uchicago.edu/print-archive/rise-nonbinding-international-agreements-empirical-comparative-and-normative-analysis.

[25] Curtis Bradley, Jack Goldsmith & Oona Hathaway, "Congress Mandates Sweeping Transparency Reforms for International Agreements" (12/23/2022), https://www.lawfaremedia.org/article/congress-mandates-sweeping-transparency-reforms-international-agreements.

Some countries do publish a treaty series, such as the *United Kingdom Treaty Series*.[26] Other countries publish treaties in an official gazette.[27] However, most researchers will not have access to these print collections. An outstanding model for making treaties available is the Australian Treaties Library.[28] To locate other such collections, consult the WorldLII collection of treaties by country[29] or country research guides. When searching the web for such collections, try searching for a website for the country's equivalent to the State Department, like a ministry or department of foreign affairs.

A few collections of bilateral treaties are freely available on the web. Many of these agreements are not translated since they are concluded by countries where English is not one of the primary languages. Some of these collections are made available by international organizations. For example, the United Nations Conference on Trade and Development (UNCTAD) produces a database of international investment treaties which includes bilateral

---

26 Treaty Series (1892–); available online as U.K. Treaties Online, https://treaties.fcdo.gov.uk/responsive/app/consolidatedSearch/.

27 Official gazettes are published by a government and are often the primary mechanism for distributing laws. Some of these publications are available on the web.

28 https://www.austlii.edu.au/au/other/dfat/.

29 http://www.worldlii.org/catalog/2322.html.

investment treaties (BITs) as well as treaties with investment provisions (TIPs).[30]

B. MULTILATERAL TREATIES

1. Indexes

Multilateral Treaties Deposited with the Secretary General (1982–) is a good source for citations and a list of the parties to an agreement. It is limited to those treaties deposited with the UN. An electronic version is also available on the UN Treaty Collection on the web.[31]

One of the most complete treaty indexes, at least for the time period covered, is Christian L. Wiktor, *Multilateral Treaty Calendar = Répertoire des Traités Multilatéraux, 1648–1995* (1998). This hefty volume provides citation information, treaty depository, and information about later related treaties and amendments. This title is searchable on HeinOnline in the World Treaty Library.

Law students in particular will want to check out this research guide—"Frequently-Cited Treaties & Other International Instruments."[32] The guide is organized by subject and provides a list of frequently cited multilateral treaties, along with available

---

30 International Investment Agreements Navigator, https://investmentpolicy.unctad.org/international-investment-agreements.

31 https://treaties.un.org/pages/ParticipationStatus.aspx?clang=_en.

32 https://libguides.law.umn.edu/frequentlycitedtreaties.

sources for the print source. A big bonus is that the citations are basically in *Bluebook* format.

2. Full-Text Sources

There are many sources for the full text of multilateral treaties, both print and electronic. Some of the primary print historical collections include the *Consolidated Treaty Series* (cited as C.T.S.) (1969–1986), which covers 1648–1918,[33] and the *League of Nations Treaty Series* (cited as L.N.T.S.) (1920–1946), which covers 1920–1944. L.N.T.S. is also available on the UN Treaty Collection database.[34]

The *United Nations Treaty Series* (cited as U.N.T.S.) covers 1944–present and is one of the most important treaty collections. Most, if not all, of the treaties contained in this source are also contained within the UN Treaty Collection website.[35]

HeinOnline offers several useful treaty databases besides the U.S. treaty collections. In the United Nations Law Collection,[36] you can search for treaties using the L.N.T.S. and U.N.T.S. citation or by other search terms. If you have a citation, try this database first, since you cannot search by U.N.T.S. citation on the UN Treaty Collection. A more comprehensive collection is the World Treaty Library, a large

---

33 Available online as Oxford Historical Treaties (OHT), https://opil.ouplaw.com/home/OHT (subscription database).

34 https://treaties.un.org/pages/LONOnline.aspx?clang=_en.

35 https://treaties.un.org/pages/AdvanceSearch.aspx?tab=UNTS&clang=_en.

36 https://heinonline.org/ (subscription database).

collection of treaty indexes and collections of treaties, like the U.S. and UN collections.[37]

Since not all treaties are deposited with the U.N., there are other international organizations that publish treaties concluded under the auspices of the organization. For example, the Council of Europe publishes the *European Treaty Series* (1949–)[38] and *European Conventions and Agreements* (1971–1999). The Organization of American States publishes a *Treaty Series* (1956–) as well.[39] Many intergovernmental organizations have websites that contain the text of these treaties.

Other sources for treaties include periodicals, loose-leaf services or subject compilations, such as *Investment Promotion and Protection Treaties* (1983–) or *International Arbitration Treaties* (3rd ed. 2010–).[40] These topical collections may also contain bilateral treaties. For example, the International Bureau of Fiscal Documentation (IBFD) has an extensive database of bilateral tax treaties.[41]

3. Status and Ratification

Once the text of the treaty has been located, the next step is to determine the parties, ratifications, and reservations. In some cases, this information can be the most difficult to locate (or to locate all of the

---

37 https://heinonline.org/ (subscription database).

38 https://www.coe.int/en/web/conventions/full-list.

39 https://www.oas.org/en/sla/dil/treaties_agreements.asp.

40 Also available on Arbitration Law (Juris), https://arbitrationlaw.com/ (subscription database).

41 https://www.ibfd.org (subscription database).

pieces of information in one place). A treaty secretariat (the treaty's administrative or executive body) or the depositary (the custodian of the treaty; may be a country or an international organization) can be the best place for current status and ratification information. The depositary is usually indicated in the final article of the treaty, and the depositary functions are detailed in Article 77 of the Vienna Convention on the Law of Treaties.

The web has become one of the most important sources for status and ratification information from treaty secretariats, national ministries, and international organizations. One of the best sources is the Multilateral Treaties Deposited with the Secretary General, part of the UN Treaty Collection.[42] Under "Status of Treaties," updated information on parties; signature and ratification dates; and reservations and declarations is available. Keep in mind that this is only for those treaties deposited with the UN. Other organizational or treaty secretariat websites provide similar information for treaties under their control, like the Council of Europe or the International Committee of the Red Cross.

"RUDs" are reservations, understandings, and declarations. Reservations exclude or modify the legal effect of treaty provisions; understandings and declarations clarify a State's position on a treaty. Reservations enable a State to participate in a treaty when it would otherwise be unwilling or unable to

---

42 https://treaties.un.org/Pages/ParticipationStatus.aspx.

participate. However, some treaties prohibit reservations or only permit specified reservations; see Articles 2(1)(d) and 19–23 of the Vienna Convention on the Law of Treaties. If reservations are not allowed, it will usually say so in the text of the treaty. For example, Article 30 of the Optional Protocol to the Convention against Torture states the following: "No reservations shall be made to the present Protocol." Declarations and understandings do not change or modify the binding nature of the treaty provisions. Many of the sources for status and ratification information also provide access to RUDs.

See Appendix C for a list of treaty collections on the web.

4.6 IMPLEMENTING LEGISLATION

Treaties may be "self-executing" (they become effective as domestic law as soon as they enter into force) or they may be non-self-executing and require "implementing legislation." Implementing legislation may require a new domestic law or changes to an existing law (technically, the legislation is the domestic law and not the treaty).

It is important to note that it is not always clear whether a treaty is self-executing or requires implementing legislation. Some treaties contain a provision calling for implementing legislation. Article VII of the Chemical Weapons Convention states that each State Party shall adopt the necessary measures to implement the convention. In the U.S., the Executive Branch often decides whether or not a treaty requires such legislation. However, on occasion, the Senate includes an understanding in the resolution of ratification stating that certain provisions are not self-executing or that the President is to exchange or deposit the instrument of ratification only after implementation legislation has been enacted.

Keep in mind that some jurisdictions always require domestic implementing legislation. There is a great deal of scholarship about concepts called monism and dualism. Basically, monists believe that international law does not need to be translated into national law. Dualists state that international law is not directly applicable domestically. This is a great simplification of these concepts. For more information, see Part IV on treaty application, in *The Oxford Guide to Treaties* (Duncan B. Hollis, ed., 2nd ed. 2020).

To locate implementing legislation, consult sources of domestic legislation for the country in question. If there is a treaty secretariat, try its website first since it may provide such information. For example, see the secretariat's website for the Chemical Weapons Convention.[43] Article VII of this convention covers national implementation measures.

4.7 BACKGROUND INFORMATION AND TREATY INTERPRETATION

Researching the background or history of non-U.S. treaties is challenging, especially for bilateral

---

[43] WPCW Legislation Database, https://www.opcw.org/resources/national-implementation/legislation-compendium.

treaties. For the most part, you will not have access to legislative history materials for other countries. If you are researching the background of a multilateral treaty, many more resources are available.

Look for "travaux préparatoires," or history and commentaries, in library catalogs or use journal indexes. Search for books and articles using the following terms: travaux, drafting, history, commentary, and document collections. For example, The *Universal Declaration of Human Rights: The Travaux Préparatoires* (William A. Schabas ed., 2013), Eileen Denza's *Diplomatic Law: A Commentary on the Vienna Convention on Diplomatic Relations* (4th ed. 2016), and "The Meaning of Investment: ICSID's Travaux and the Domain of International Investment Law," 51 *Harvard Int'l L.J.* 257 (2010).[44]

For more information on how to research the history of a treaty, see "À la Recherche des Travaux Préparatoires: An Approach to Researching the Drafting History of International Agreements" by Jonathan Pratter.[45] The Yale Law Library has also prepared a handy list of collected travaux préparatoires.[46] While this list does not always link to an electronic collection, it's useful to know if

---

44 Available on HeinOnline, https://heinonline.org/ (subscription database).

45 https://www.nyulawglobal.org/globalex/Travaux_Preparatoires1.html.

46 https://library.law.yale.edu/research-guides/collected-travaux-preparatoires.

something is available in print. They have also included the tables of contents for the print sources.

If the treaty or agreement was concluded pursuant to an international conference, look for conference documents using the name of the conference as an author or subject in a library catalog. If it is a recent conference, try searching for the conference on the web. For example, the United Nations Framework Convention on Climate Change website provides access to documents, national reports, and other up-to-date information.[47]

The International Law Commission (ILC) is the body responsible for codifying written international law (treaties). Therefore, the ILC website contains draft documents, commentary, and other relevant information on treaties done under its mandate.[48] Another interesting collection from the UN is the Audiovisual Library of International Law. The Historic Archives focuses on specific legal instruments (treaties and agreements) and includes an introduction prepared by an international legal scholar, a procedural history, and related documents for each listed instrument.[49]

If the treaty or conference was done under the auspices of an international organization, such as the UN, look for documents using tools for locating such

---

[47] https://unfccc.int/.

[48] https://legal.un.org/ilc/texts/texts.shtml.

[49] https://legal.un.org/avl/historicarchives.html.

documents. See the United Nations Documentation Research Guide from Dag Hammarskjold Library[50].

If you want to research how treaties are implemented or interpreted in domestic legal systems, look for books and articles on "treaty-making power," such as *National Treaty Law and Practice Canada, Egypt, Israel, Mexico, Russia, South Africa* (2003). International law yearbooks are also good sources for how a specific country has implemented and interpreted international law. See Chapter 5 of this *Nutshell* for more information on yearbooks.

International courts are very useful for interpretation and analysis of treaties. Useful sources include international law yearbooks, *International Law Reports* (1919–) (a compilation of selected international and domestic court decisions),[51] and the Oxford Reports on International Law database (selected international and domestic case law on international legal issues).[52]

U.S. lawyers will also want to consult *Restatement of the Law, Fourth, Foreign Relations Law of the United States* (2018–). This is a very useful source for

---

[50] https://research.un.org/en.

[51] Available on vLex, https://vlex.com (subscription database).

[52] Available at https://opil.ouplaw.com/home/oril (subscription database).

locating relevant cases and secondary sources on treaty interpretation and analysis.[53]

4.8 FINAL THOUGHTS

Here are some final thoughts on treaty research.

1) Read the treaty; it provides important details on these issues:
   - Entry into force
   - Depositary/Secretariat
   - Implementing legislation needed
   - Other conditions
2) You may need to use more than one source for locating or researching the following:
   - Complete text of the treaty
   - Legal citation
   - Status and RUDs
   - Legislative history information
   - Sources for interpretation and analysis

---

[53] Available on Lexis, Westlaw, and HeinOnline. The new edition does not entirely replace the *Restatement, Third,* so consulting both may be necessary.

CHAPTER 5

CUSTOMARY INTERNATIONAL LAW AND GENERAL PRINCIPLES OF LAW

5.1 INTRODUCTION

According to Article 38(1)(b) and (c) of the International Court of Justice Statute, customary international law and general principles of law are two of the major sources of international law. Neither of these "sources of law" will sound familiar to a non-specialist. But if you consider the matter for a second, they are natural locations for authority in international law. Nations have been dealing with each other for millennia. For all the faults that one can find with international law, an amazing amount of international law has worked fine for centuries. Travel, trade, communications, and diplomacy, the list could go on and on. It makes sense that some of these deep-rooted concepts have taken on the force of law. Perhaps no one can pinpoint when a custom began, or when it became accepted. The important point is that it is accepted as the governing rule.

This type of authority is not so different from the idea of common law; it is just more complex because it springs from the interaction of many nations and traditions. Nor is it always clear just what customary international law and general principles of law might be. Naturally, these are also the two most difficult sources to research. They are documented in a wide variety of sources and often involve very subjective evaluation. This Chapter will try to help guide you, but in this area, asking for help from a librarian or a more experienced researcher may be the best solution.

Article 38(1)(d) also mentions judicial decisions and the teachings of publicists as "subsidiary means for the determination of rules of law." Case law and teachings are not primary sources of law, but they do provide evidence of the primary sources of international law. These forms of authority are familiar to the modern American researcher and knowing which publicists (meaning scholarly commentators) are central is just a matter of learning about them. I will provide a list of the most widely accepted sources at the end of this Chapter. For more information on customary international law, see Tullio Treves, "Customary International Law," in *Max Planck Encyclopedias of International Law* (2006).[1] This chapter covers the theory and practice of customary international law.

5.2 CUSTOMARY INTERNATIONAL LAW

Some basic definitions will help. Customary international law "consists of rules of law derived

---

1 https://opil.ouplaw.com/home/mpil (subscription database).

from the consistent conduct of States acting out of the belief that the law required them to act that way."[2] The elements of customary international law include:

- Widespread repetition by States of similar international acts over time, referred to as "state practice." In other words, "everyone has always done it this way."
- Acts must occur out of a sense of obligation, called *opinio juris*. In other words, "everyone has always done it this way because they knew they were supposed to do so."
- Norms that a significant number of states follow and few states reject. Of course, there is no magic number here. In other words, "when we say everyone, we mean everyone."

The *Restatement (Fourth) of Foreign Relations* states in a straightforward manner: "[c]ustomary international law results from a general and consistent practice of states followed by them from a sense of legal obligation."[3]

"Customary international law develops from the practice of States. To international lawyers, 'the practice of states' means official governmental conduct reflected in a variety of acts, including official statements at international conferences and in diplomatic exchanges, formal instructions to

---

[2] Shabtai Rosenne, *Practice and Methods of International Law* 55 (1984).

[3] *Restatement of the Law, Fourth, the Foreign Relations Law of the United States*, § 102 (2018, annual supplements), available on Lexis, Westlaw, and HeinOnline.

diplomatic agents, national court decisions, legislative measures, or other actions taken by governments to deal with matters of international concern."[4]

A particular category of customary rules is called *jus cogens*, or peremptory norms. These rules are considered universal, and no derogation is allowed. Of course, there is no definitive list of such norms, but this list usually includes the following: prohibitions of aggression, genocide, slavery, racial discrimination, crimes against humanity and torture, and the right to self-determination.[5]

Customary international law is difficult to research. The sources are scattered, not well indexed, may lack legal terminology, and may only be available in the vernacular. Secondary sources are the best source for locating evidence of customary international law.

The outline for the research process looks like this:

1. Basic reference tools (encyclopedias and dictionaries, see Chapter 2)
2. Writings of publicists (commentary and analysis, see Chapter 10)
    - Books
    - Articles

---

[4] Thomas Buergenthal & Sean Murphy, *Public International Law in a Nutshell* 27 (6th ed. 2019).

[5] For more information on these norms, see Dire Tladi, "Ius Cogens," in *Max Planck Encyclopedias of International Law* (2024), https://opil.ouplaw.com (subscription database).

3. International law decisions (see Chapter 6)
4. Treaties and agreements (see Chapter 4)
5. State practice
6. IGO practice (international governmental organizations)
7. National laws (see Chapter 3)
8. Fact-based research (depending on the topic)

The focus of the rest of this chapter is on researching State practice and general principles.

5.3 STATE PRACTICE

When researching customary international law, the objective is to find evidence of the relevant State practice. Evidence of State practice is found in a variety of primary source materials. In 1950, the International Law Commission listed the following as evidence of customary international law: treaties, decisions of national and international courts, national legislation, opinions of national legal advisors, diplomatic correspondence, and practice of international organizations. This list, which was not intended to be exhaustive, is a useful starting point and a basis for discussion.[6]

---

[6] "Report of the International Law Commission to the General Assembly (Part II): Ways and Means of Making the Evidence of Customary International Law More Readily Available," [1950] 2 *Y.B. Int'l L. Comm'n* 367, ILC Doc. A/1316, https://legal.un.org/ilc/documentation/english/reports/a_cn4_34.pdf.

One of the best sources of State practice is the records of a State's foreign relations and diplomatic practices. However, while it is tradition to produce such publications, the information can be quite difficult to obtain because many states do not make it available to the public. It may come as a surprise to the neophyte that such compilations exist at all. For the U.S., the best source is the series called *Foreign Relations of the United States* (FRUS) (1861–), which "presents the official documentary historical record of major U.S. foreign policy decisions and significant diplomatic activity."[7] The series began in 1861 and consists of hundreds of individual volumes. The volumes contain documents from Presidential libraries, the Departments of State and Defense, the National Security Council, the Central Intelligence Agency, the Agency for International Development, and other foreign affairs agencies. It also contains the private papers of individuals involved in formulating U.S. foreign policy. The series represents an amazingly detailed account of the international activity of the U.S. You will not be surprised to discover that this set appears with elegant slowness. Reagan administration documents are still under declassification review and the Bush and Clinton administrations are being researched and reviewed.

---

7 https://history.state.gov/historicaldocuments/.

Researchers can now obtain many of these volumes on the web from the State Department's Office of the Historian[8] and from HeinOnline.

Other, more current documents and bits of information are available in the *Department of State Bulletin* (1939–1989) and the *Dispatch* (1990–1999). Both publications contain documentation and information from the Department of State and provide a wealth of information on foreign relations. Unfortunately, the State Department discontinued publication of these sources in 1999. The same information that was contained in the two former tools is supposedly available on the website of the State Department, but locating it is now more challenging.[9]

A good source for locating sources of State practice for many countries is *Sources of State Practice in International Law* (Gaebler & Shea, eds., 2nd rev. ed. 2014). For each country included in this volume, there is information on treaty collections, diplomatic and state papers, and other sources. This is a fine place to start, but it may lack current web resources since it was published in 2014.

Many countries have websites for departments or ministries that serve the same function as the U.S. Department of State, e.g. the United Kingdom's Foreign, Commonwealth & Development Office,[10]

---

8 https://history.state.gov/historicaldocuments/about-frus.

9 https://www.state.gov/.

10 https://www.gov.uk/government/organisations/foreign-commonwealth-development-office.

Australia's Department of Foreign Affairs and Trade,[11] and Germany's Auswärtiges Amt [Federal Foreign Office].[12] What you find at each site will vary.

International law digests are another useful source. Digests aid in locating customary international law contained in diplomatic papers of States. The easiest to access are the digests for the U.S. For historical information, there are many digests covering the late 19th century and the 20th century: Cadwalader, *Digest of Published Opinions of the Attorneys-General and of the Leading Decisions of the Federal Courts, with Reference to International Law, Treaties, and Kindred Subjects* (1877); Wharton, *Digest of the International Law of the United States* (1886); Moore, *Digest of International Law* (1906); Hackworth, *Digest of International Law* (1940–1944); and Whiteman, *Digest of International Law* (1963–1973). These digests are also available on HeinOnline.[13]

More contemporary information can be located in the *Digest of United States Practice in International Law* (1973–1980; 2001–).[14] The earlier edition was continued by *Cumulative Digest of United States Practice in International Law* (1981–) which covered 1981–1988. These volumes were supplemented monthly by a column in the *American Journal of*

---

11 https://www.dfat.gov.au/.

12 https://www.auswaertiges-amt.de/de/.

13 https://heinonline.org (subscription database).

14 https://www.state.gov/digest-of-united-states-practice-in-international-law/. Also available on HeinOnline, https://heinonline.org/ (subscription database).

International Law ("Contemporary Practice of the United States Relating to International Law"). The new edition of the *Digest* began with 2000 and is issued annually. Documents listed in the *Digest* are available on the State Department's website.[15] Sean Murphy produces another digest: *United States Practice in International Law* (2002–). This publication includes citations to U.S. statutes and cases, U.S. documents, international documents, and other materials. Unfortunately, there are only two volumes in this series, covering 1999–2004.

While the sources noted above are important for researching customary international law, probably the best resource for U.S. legal researchers is the *Restatement of the Law, Fourth, Foreign Relations* (2018–, plus supplement).[16] Like all *Restatements*, it is the distillation of the best thinking of scholars, judges, and lawyers. Though it is unofficial, it possesses great authority with a focus on the U.S. and cites other international documents. If you do nothing else, go to this *Restatement* to gain a better understanding of customary international law. The *Restatement* is a reliable source of context, and it is designed to be a rational explanation of the field.

A country's domestic laws also provide evidence of international custom because they indicate the State's practice and obligations. To research the law

---

15 https://www.state.gov/digest-of-united-states-practice-in-international-law/.

16 Also available on Westlaw, Lexis, and HeinOnline. Note that the *Fourth Restatement* is not yet complete, so consult the *Third Restatement* as well.

of other countries, see Chapter 3 of this *Nutshell*. Because locating the laws relevant to international law can be a daunting task, you should use a "yearbook" if one is available for the jurisdiction. Many countries publish an international yearbook that contains summaries or overviews of national legislation and case law dealing with that State's international obligations. These yearbooks may include cases involving questions of public international law, legislation concerning matters of international law, practice in international law, and treaty actions. At this point, you will not be surprised to learn that most yearbooks lag years behind. These examples may give you an idea of the breadth of yearbooks, but there are many more available:

- *African Yearbook of International Law = Annuaire Africain de Droit International* (1994–).[17]
- *Annuaire Français de Droit International* (1955–).
- *Asian Yearbook of International Law* (1993–).[18]
- *Australian Yearbook of International Law* (1966–).[19]

---

[17] Also available on HeinOnline, https://heinonline.org/ (subscription database) and Brill Online, https://brill.com/view/journals/afyo/afyo-overview.xml (subscription databases).

[18] Also available on HeinOnline, https://heinonline.org/ (subscription database).

[19] Also available on HeinOnline, https://heinonline.org/ (subscription database).

- *German Yearbook of International Law* (1948–).[20]
- *Japanese Annual of International Law* (1957–2007). Continued by the *Japanese Yearbook of International Law* (2009–).[21]
- *Netherlands Yearbook of International Law* (1970–).
- *Russian Yearbook of International Law* (1994–).
- *Spanish Yearbook of International Law* (1994–).[22]

Intergovernmental organizations also publish yearbooks that provide an annual survey of the organization's activities as well as State practice. Evidence of State practice can be found in documents issued by intergovernmental organizations, such as resolutions and declarations. Resolutions are non-binding, but they reflect the acceptance of international norms. A useful way to locate this information is to use an organization's annual yearbook. Some common yearbooks include the *Max Planck Yearbook of United Nations Law* (1998–)[23]

---

[20] Also available on HeinOnline, https://heinonline.org/ (subscription database).

[21] Also available on HeinOnline, https://heinonline.org/ (subscription database).

[22] Also available on HeinOnline, https://heinonline.org/ (subscription database) and Brill Online, https://brill.com/view/journals/syio/syio-overview.xml (vols. 1–17) (subscription databases). Freely available at https://www.sybil.es/sybil/index.

[23] Also available on HeinOnline, https://heinonline.org/ (subscription database).

and the United Nations International Law Commission, *Yearbook of the International Law Commission* (1949–).[24]

For a good list of yearbooks, see Renu Urvashi Sagreiya, "Researching Customary International Law, State Practice, and the Pronouncements of States Regarding International Law" (2024).[25]

Along with yearbooks, some countries may have individual volumes on practice or an annual series. Some examples include *Indian Practice of International Law: Global Norms and their Domestic Enforcement* (Siddhartha Misra ed., 2024) or *German Practice in International Law* (Stefan Talmon ed., 2022—).[26] Be on the lookout for materials on state practice that focus on a specific jurisdiction and topics, such as Stellina Jolly & Nafees Ahmad, *Climate Refugees in South Asia: Protection Under International Legal Standards and State Practices in South Asia* (2019).

There are a few published sources that compile State practice and, if one exists on your topic, it can be an enormously helpful source. Some of these include *State Practice Regarding State Immunities* (2006)[27]; *Customary International Humanitarian Law* (2005) (a detailed, three-volume set: Volume 1

---

24 https://legal.un.org/ilc/publications/yearbooks/.

25 https://www.nyulawglobal.org/globalex/Customary_International_Law1.html#international-yearbooks.

26 Although this series was first published in 2022, the first volume covers practice in 2019.

27 Also available on Brill Online, https://brill.com/view/title/12589?language=en (subscription database).

contains the rules and Volumes 2 & 3 contain examples of State practice)[28]; *Targeted Killing in International Law* (2009); *The Persistent Objector Rule in International Law* (2016); and *The Formation and Identification of Rules of Customary International Law in International Investment Law* (2016). Compilations like these may be available for other topics in journal literature. For example, I.M. Siatitsa & M. Titberidze, "Human Rights in Armed Conflict: Ten Years of Affirmative State Practice within United Nations Resolutions," 3 *J. Int'l Humanitarian Legal Stud.* 233 (2012). A 2014 paper by Joel P. Trachtman contains a handy chart of 300 rules of customary international law and the sources for the rules.[29] Check the periodical indexes discussed in Chapter 10 to find such articles.

Some journals have begun to collect State practice and publish this information in selected issues. *The Journal on the Use of Force and International Law* (2014–)[30] provides a Digest of State Practice "which will act as a key means of assessing the development of customary international law in the area."[31] Another example is from the *Asia-Pacific Journal of*

---

28 Available and updated on the ICRC Customary IHL database, https://ihl-databases.icrc.org/en/customary-ihl.

29 Joel P. Trachtman, "The Obsolescence of Customary International Law" (October 21, 2014). Available at SSRN: https://ssrn.com/abstract=2512757 or http://dx.doi.org/10.2139/ssrn.2512757.

30 Also available at https://www.tandfonline.com/journals/rjuf20 (subscription database).

31 https://www.tandfonline.com/ (subscription database).

Ocean Law and Policy (2016–).[32] It contains a section called "State Law of the Sea Practice in Asian Pacific States" and provides brief summaries of developments in national practice related to law of the sea issues. And, finally, see the *Yearbook of International Environmental Law* (1990–),[33] the year in review section examines the practice of States and international organizations on a variety of international environmental law topics.

5.4 GENERAL PRINCIPLES

Article 38 of the International Court of Justice Statute includes "general principles of law recognized by civilized nations" as another source of international law. General principles are basic concepts of fairness and justice applied universally in legal systems around the world (e.g. laches, good faith, res judicata, impartiality of judges). They frequently involve procedural matters. International tribunals rely on these principles when they cannot find authority in other sources of international law. As stated by many legal scholars, general principles "fill the gap" when no treaty or custom exits to resolve an international dispute.[34] To make this a bit more clear, Professor Janis states:

---

[32] Available on Brill Online, https://brill.com/view/journals/apoc/apoc-overview.xml (subscription database).

[33] https://academic.oup.com/yielaw/ (subscription database).

[34] Yilin Wang, "The Origins and Operation of the General Principles of Law as Gap Fillers," 13 *J. Int'l Dispute Settlement* 560–582 (2022), https://doi.org/10.1093/jnlids/idac018.

> "The basic notion is that a general principle of international law is some proposition of law so fundamental that it will be found in virtually every legal system. When treaties and customary international law fail to offer a needed international rule, a search may be launched in comparative law to discover if national legal systems use a common legal principle. If such a common legal principle is found, then it is presumed that a comparable principle should be attributed to fill the gap in international law."[35]

For the most part, there is no handy list of these principles, but you can find references in decisions of international tribunals and national courts and in the writings (or teachings) of publicists. There are a few sources that provide information on general principles: see Bin Cheng, *General Principles of Law, as applied by International Courts and Tribunals* (1953); *General Principles of Law in the Decisions of International Criminal Courts and Tribunals* (2008)[36]; *General Principles and the Coherence of International Law* (2019); and *General Principles of Law Recognized by Civilized Nations (1922–2018): The Evolution of the Third Source of International Law Through the Jurisprudence of the Permanent Court of International Justice and the International Court of Justice* (2020).

---

[35] Mark W. Janis, *An Introduction to International Law* 55 (4th ed. 2003).

[36] Available on Brill Online, https://brill.com/view/title/15490 (subscription database).

Article 38 also mentions "judicial decisions and the teachings of the most highly qualified publicists of the various nations, as subsidiary means for the determination of rules of law." These sources are generally the best place to start researching an international law topic since they can help you identify rules in other sources of international law, such as treaties. Scholarly works include treatises, journal articles, publications of scholarly associations, and articles in encyclopedias.

The writings of publicists can be found in most law libraries and even in non-specialized collections. As with general principles, there is no official list of who is considered a publicist and who is not. The most prominent specialists will vary from topic to topic. However, here are some recognized classics:

Bowett's Law of International Institutions (Philippe Sands; Pierre Klein; D.W. Bowett, eds., 6th ed. 2009).

Andrew Clapman, *Brierly's Law of Nations: An Introduction to the International Law of Peace* (7th ed. 2012).

James Crawford, *Brownlie's Principles of Public International Law* (9th ed. 2019).

Oppenheim's International Law: United Nations (Rosalyn Higgins et al., eds., 2017).

Malcolm N. Shaw, *International Law* (9th ed. 2021).

Max Planck Encyclopedias of International Law.[37]

Many of these important books are available from Oxford Scholarly Authorities database.[38] A very useful tool for locating more scholarly works by topic is Oxford Bibliographies Online: International Law, which contains abstracts and citations to both books and articles on international law.[39] You should also look at the *Collected Course of the Hague Academy of International Law*.[40] This collection contains the lectures given by well-recognized international law scholars (these folks are considered publicists as noted in Article 38(1)(d) of the ICJ statute).

A question that often comes up is how you determine if a specific author or scholar is considered a "publicist." If you are unsure, look at the author's credentials and the list of their publications on the website of their affiliated institution or organization. Many authors have an ORCID ID[41] which will contain professional information as well as publications. HeinOnline also provides author

---

37 https://opil.ouplaw.com/home/MPIL (subscription database).

38 http://opil.ouplaw.com/home/OSAIL (subscription database).

39 http://www.oxfordbibliographies.com/ (subscription database).

40 Available in print and online, HeinOnline, https://hein online.org/ (subscription database) and Brill Online, https:// referenceworks.brillonline.com/subjects/Law (subscription databases).

41 https://orcid.org/.

profiles with a list of their publications (at least the ones available on HeinOnline).[42]

Judicial decisions are good for finding references to and recognition of rules in other sources of law, such as treaties. To locate the decisions of international courts and tribunals, see Chapter 6.

When looking for general principles contained in articles or in decisions, search the text of these materials using the following phrases: "established principle"; "general concept of law"; "general principle"; "universal or absolute principle of international law"; "all systems of law"; or "established rule of law."

Also consider searching for [your CIL concept] within the same sentence of custom OR "international custom" OR "customary international law." Using the terms "state practice" may also be useful when searching for books and articles.

Here are a few examples using the methodologies noted above:

Xuexia Liao, "The LOSC as a Package Deal and Its Implications for Determination of Customary International Law," 35 *Int'l J. Marine and Coastal L.* 704 (2020).[43]

---

[42] "Author Profiles" are available from the Law Journal Library on HeinOnline, https://heinonline.org/ (subscription database).

[43] https://doi.org/10.1163/15718085-BJA10021.

María-Teresa Gil-Bazo, "Asylum as a General Principle of International Law," 27 *Int'l J Refugee Law* 3 (2015).[44]

Ilia Maria Siatitsa & Maia Titberidze, "Human Rights in Armed Conflict: Ten Years of Affirmative State Practice within United Nations Resolutions," 3 *J. Int'l Humanitarian Legal Stud.* 233 (2012).[45]

For more assistance with researching customary international law and general principles, try using another guide called "Researching Customary International Law, State Practice and the Pronouncements of States regarding International Law" by Renu Urvashi Sagreiya.[46]

As a final thought, never hesitate to ask for help. A reference librarian who works with international materials may be able to point you in the right direction, saving you time and energy. This is an area where there is no substitute for expertise.

---

44 https://doi.org/10.1093/ijrl/eeu062.

45 https://doi.org/10.1163/18781527-00302007.

46 https://www.nyulawglobal.org/globalex/Customary_International_Law1.html.

CHAPTER 6

INTERNATIONAL CASE LAW

6.1 INTRODUCTION

Judicial decisions are the bread and butter of research for the American legal researcher. The same is not true for research in international law. Since there is no single source of authority to enforce the judgments of an international court or tribunal, international case law has never been as central to the research enterprise. As globalization continues to increase, the role for international decision-making bodies has grown in response.

Thus, it is not surprising that dispute resolution mechanisms have become of great interest to the international legal researcher. The novice researcher must recognize that there are a variety of bodies involved in solving international disputes: international courts and tribunals, arbitral bodies, and other quasi-judicial bodies. Some look familiar; some do not. Some of these mechanisms are developed for a particular dispute or event, and others are prescribed based on a topic, organization, or international body. Both States and individuals may bring matters before some of these bodies. Most have jurisdiction based on authority outlined in an international agreement. With each tribunal or court that you examine, you will have to turn a new page and be sure that you understand what you are working with in each instance. It is worth noting, too, that there is much discussion on the effectiveness of these bodies.

Interest in the body of case law from international courts and tribunals has increased over the years, and the tools for accessing this information have developed as well. This chapter will review the tools available for researching the major dispute settlement bodies as well as resources for accessing cases from multiple courts and tribunals.

6.2 JUDICIAL DECISIONS OF INTERNATIONAL TRIBUNALS

There is really only one court with general jurisdiction that, at least in theory, runs throughout all of the nations of the word—the International

Court of Justice (ICJ) and its predecessor, the Permanent Court of International Justice (PCIJ). Keep in mind that no entity can enforce the judgments of these courts.

A. PERMANENT COURT OF INTERNATIONAL JUSTICE (PCIJ)

The PCIJ operated from 1922–1946, and it heard 56 cases, including 29 "contentious cases" between States and 27 "advisory opinions."[1] While there is a large print collection containing all the relevant documents, the ICJ website contains all of the PCIJ documents that used to be available only in print.[2]

Selected cases from the PCIJ are also available from the WorldLII Project on International Courts & Tribunals.[3] The advantage of this database over the ICJ website is its superior search mechanism. Information about the PCIJ is also available on another website called Worldcourts.[4] This site also has decisions, including judgments, advisory opinions, and orders.

B. INTERNATIONAL COURT OF JUSTICE (ICJ)

"The Court has a twofold role: to settle, in accordance with international law, legal disputes submitted to it by States ([c]ontentious cases) and to give advisory opinions ([a]dvisory procedures) on

---

1 https://www.icj-cij.org/en/pcij.

2 Series A–F and other documents, https://www.icj-cij.org/en/pcij.

3 http://www.worldlii.org/int/cases/PCIJ/.

4 https://www.worldcourts.com/pcij/eng/index.htm.

legal questions referred to it by duly authorized United Nations organs and specialized agencies."[5] The ICJ website contains all of the decisions of the Court. Five series of publications are accessible on the site (as well as in print): 1) Reports of Judgments, Advisory Opinions and Orders; 2) Pleadings, Oral Arguments, Documents; 3) Acts and Documents; 4) Yearbooks; and 5) Bibliography. Basic documents, such as the Statute and Rules of the Court, are also available on this site.

The Dag Hammarskjold Library has a very useful research guide outlining the functions of the Court, as well as the documentation.[6] The decisions and documents are also available on Westlaw and Lexis. These databases may not be as current as the ICJ website, but they do provide more advanced search capabilities.

There is a considerable amount of commentary and analysis on the ICJ. Some of the most notable ones include: *The Statute of the International Court of Justice: A Commentary* (Andreas Zimmermann et al. eds., 3rd ed. 2019); *Rosenne's Law and Practice of the International Court: 1920–2015* (5th ed. 2016)[7]; *The Elgar Companion to the International Court of Justice* (Robert Kolb, 2014); and Inna Uchkunova, *World Court Practice Guide: Summaries and Index of PCIJ and ICJ Cases* (2016).

---

5 https://www.icj-cij.org/en/cases.

6 https://research.un.org/en/docs/icj.

7 Available online at Brill Online, https://brill.com/view/db/rose (subscription database).

For more information on researching the United Nations, see Chapter 8.

C. COURT OF JUSTICE OF THE EUROPEAN UNION (CJEU/ECJ)

The European Court of Justice is the highest legal authority in the EU. The Court is empowered to interpret and apply the foundational EU treaties. Unlike the ICJ, this Court can enforce its decisions. EU institutions and Member States may appeal and take each other to court for failure to implement or properly apply the treaties and secondary legislation (for example, the Commission can file a case against a Member State for not implementing a directive). The Court will also issue prejudicial decisions in cases referred to it by national courts when questions of EU law are involved. The Court is assisted by advocate-generals, who present a reasoned and independent opinion of the issue of law in the case. While there is no formal doctrine of *stare decisis* applied to these opinions, the Court tends to follow its own decisions. The decisions are binding on the national courts of Member States.

The Court's website (called Curia[8]) provides access to all case law since 1953. The European Court of Justice is comprised of two courts: the Court of Justice and the General Court (created in 1988). The Civil Service Tribunal was created in 2004 but merged into the General Court in 2016. Curia maintains records for all three institutions. The

---

[8] https://curia.europa.eu/jcms/jcms/j_6/en/.

Court's website provides access to cases by number or through an advanced search form.[9] Cases can also be searched using EUR-Lex[10] (covered in Chapter 7). Some tools on the Court's site for locating cases are only available in French.

The judgments from the Court of Justice and the General Court are available in the official *European Court Reports* series (ECR), the Court's website, Lexis, Westlaw, and vLex.[11]

D. EUROPEAN COURT OF HUMAN RIGHTS (ECtHR)

The most active of all the human rights courts and bodies is the European Court of Human Rights (ECtHR). The ECHR enforces the obligations of the Contracting States to the European Convention on Human Rights (ECHR). Initially, there were three institutions entrusted with this responsibility: the European Commission of Human Rights (1954–1998); the European Court of Human Rights (1959–); and the Committee of Ministers of the Council of Europe. Complaints were examined by the Commission, and, if declared admissible, the case was referred to the Court. If the case was not admissible, the Committee of Ministers decided whether there had been a violation of the Convention and, if appropriate, awarded "just satisfaction" to the victim. Protocol No. 11, which came into force on

---

9 https://curia.europa.eu/juris/recherche.jsf?language=en.

10 https://eur-lex.europa.eu/collection/eu-law/eu-case-law.html.

11 See Appendix A.

November 1, 1998, replaced the existing, part-time Court and Commission with a single, full-time Court.[12]

The ECtHR has an excellent website containing basic texts, cases, annual reports, and other information. The case law is contained in a database called HUDOC.[13] This is the most comprehensive collection of decisions from the Commission and the Court. You can search by words in the text of the decisions, treaty article, countries involved, and keyword. With the keyword feature, you can search using a controlled vocabulary, which will save you a lot of headaches since you won't be searching using the wrong terminology.

Another handy feature of this database is the "case details" tab for each case. This tab provides a nice rundown on the basics of the case, including information on the Convention articles at issue, the case law cited, and any other relevant international law the Court used in its decision.

The Court's website provides information about the Court and its functions. Most importantly, there are very useful tools for accessing case-law and analysis. These tools include the Knowledge Sharing (ECHR-KS) platform[14] and includes case-law guides,

---

[12] https://www.coe.int/en/web/conventions/full-list?module=treaty-detail&treatynum=155.

[13] https://www.echr.coe.int/hudoc-database.

[14] https://www.echr.coe.int/knowledge-sharing#.

summaries and other information tools organized by treaty articles.

Besides the European system, there are two other human rights systems with formal dispute settlement mechanisms—the Inter-American system and the African system. While each has its own body of decisions, none are as active as the European system. There are also several quasi-judicial bodies in the UN human rights system. These bodies issue quite a bit of jurisprudence. For more details on researching this court and international human rights law, see the Berkeley Law research guide, "International Human Rights Law."[15]

E. PERMANENT COURT OF ARBITRATION (PCA)

This Court has evolved over the years to deal with disputes between States, intergovernmental organizations, and private parties in matters of both public and private international law. It was established by the Convention for the Pacific Settlement of International Disputes, concluded at The Hague in 1899 during the first Hague Peace Conference. The PCA website provides the text of founding and basic documents.[16] It also contains access to the treaties and agreements that refer to the PCA in the body of the text.

PCA decisions are available from a variety of print and electronic sources. Past and pending cases are

---

15 https://libguides.law.berkeley.edu/c.php?g=326748.

16 https://pca-cpa.org/en/home/.

available on its website through the PCA Case section.[17] For more help with researching international arbitration, see the Berkeley Law research guide on this topic.[18]

There are other dispute settlement bodies in the area of arbitration. Two of the most prolific are the International Centre for Settlement of Investment Disputes (ICSID)[19] and the United Nations Convention on Contracts for the International Sale of Goods (CISG).[20] These bodies and many other useful resources are covered in the international arbitration research guide noted above.

F. OTHER INTERNATIONAL COURTS AND TRIBUNALS

There are several other international courts and tribunals, all which issue decisions relevant to a variety of international research topics. Below is a list of some of the courts/tribunals, with relevant links provided.

- Extraordinary Chambers in the Courts of Cambodia (ECCC).[21]
- Inter-American Court of Human Rights (IACtHR).[22]

---

17 https://pca-cpa.org/en/cases/.

18 https://libguides.law.berkeley.edu/c.php?g=326736.

19 https://icsid.worldbank.org/.

20 https://iicl.law.pace.edu/cisg/cisg.

21 https://www.eccc.gov.kh/en.

22 https://www.corteidh.or.cr/index.cfm?lang=en.

- International Criminal Court (ICC).[23]
- International Criminal Tribunal for Rwanda (ICTR).[24]
- International Criminal Tribunal for the Former Yugoslavia (ICTY).[25]
- International Tribunal for the Law of the Sea (ITLOS).[26]
- Residual Special Court for Sierra Leone.[27]
- UN Assistance to the Khmer Rouge Trials (UNAKRT).[28]
- World Trade Organization, Dispute Settlement.[29]

As mentioned throughout this *Nutshell*, search for a research guide on the court/tribunal or the topic handled by the court to learn more about how to locate decisions and other documents issued by these

---

23 https://www.icc-cpi.int.

24 https://unictr.irmct.org/. While this court is no longer active, the caselaw is still relevant. See also, https://www.irmct.org/en, the International Residual Mechanism for Criminal Tribunals. The Mechanism carries out a number of functions previously handled by the ICTR and ICTY.

25 https://www.icty.org/. While this court is no longer active, the caselaw is still relevant. See also, https://www.irmct.org/en, the International Residual Mechanism for Criminal Tribunals. The Mechanism carries out a number of functions previously handled by the ICTR and ICTY.

26 https://www.itlos.org/.

27 https://www.rscsl.org/.

28 https://www.unakrt-online.org.

29 https://www.wto.org/english/tratop_e/dispu_e/dispu_e.htm.

bodies. You can find a guide for any of the bodies mentioned in this chapter (and more). The Harvard Law Library guide on "International Courts and Tribunals" is a good way to get some basic information about many courts and tribunals (African Court of Justice, Iran-US Claims Tribunal, ITLOS, etc.) and includes books and relevant research guides.[30]

6.3 OTHER USEFUL WEBSITES AND DATABASES

The WorldLII International Courts & Tribunals Collection is a website that provides searchable access to the decisions of many international courts and tribunals.[31] The site aims to provide a comprehensive search facility for final decisions of all international and multi-national courts and tribunals, whether global or regional. You may search this site as a whole or select individual databases. Of course, the coverage offered for each court or tribunal varies, so check the "Update Status for International Decisions" page on this website. Another similar collection is called Worldcourts, an international case law database from more than 50 institutions, including the Caribbean Court of Justice, the Human Rights Committee, and the International Criminal Court.[32] The scope of the database is available on the website.

---

30 https://guides.library.harvard.edu/law/international courts.

31 http://www.worldlii.org/int/cases/.

32 https://worldcourts.com/.

As noted above, there is no one site that provides access to all of the decisions from international courts and tribunals. The same is true of print sources. *International Law Reports* (1919–)[33] contains full-text cases, translated into English, from both national (on international law issues) and international tribunals. However, the coverage is selective, and the translations take some time. It is a fairly good source for locating older cases.

Oxford University Press also offers a database called Oxford Reports on International law.[34] This database is a collection of more than 5,500 public international law cases from international courts, national (domestic) courts, and ad hoc tribunals. Cases are selected by local reporters and contain the following features: analytical commentary; full texts of judgments in the original language; and English translations of a number of the key decisions.

Cambridge Law Reports is another database containing international law cases. Coverage includes the cases from *International Law Reports* (1919–) and *ICSID Reports: Reports of Cases Decided under the Convention on the Settlement of Investment Disputes between States and Nationals of Other States, 1965* (1993–).[35]

---

[33] Previous titles were *Annual Digest of Public International Law Cases and Annual Digest* and *Reports of Public International Law Cases*. Also available electronically on the vLex database (subscription database).

[34] https://opil.ouplaw.com/home/oril (subscription database).

[35] https://www.cambridge.org/core/publications/collections/cambridge-law-reports-collection (subscription database).

Most other collections of decisions focus on particular topics, like arbitration, trade law, human rights, and international criminal law. Some collections provide access to national court opinions on these international law topics. Here's a sampling of a few topical collections:

Arbitration/Trade

- Case Law on UNCITRAL Texts (CLOUT).[36]
- Investment Treaty Arbitration (italaw).[37]
- Investor-State LawGuide.[38]
- TradeLawGuide (WTO case law).[39]

Human Rights and Related Topics

- African Child Rights Cases, a collection of judgments from domestic courts in various African countries on cases related to the rights and welfare of children.[40]
- African Human Rights Case Law Analyser, a collection of human rights decisions from various African bodies.[41]

---

36 https://uncitral.un.org/en/case_law.

37 https://www.italaw.com/.

38 https://new.investorstatelawguide.com/ (subscription database).

39 https://www.tradelawguide.com (subscription database).

40 https://www.acerwc.africa/en/resources/case-law-database.

41 https://caselaw.ihrda.org/.

- Inter-American Court of Human Rights Project, access to decisions rendered by the Inter-American Court of Human Rights.[42]
- Refworld (UNHCR), Case Law Collection (refugee related case law from national and international courts and tribunals).[43]

International Criminal Law

- Annotated Leading Cases of International Criminal Tribunals, texts and commentary of leading cases from ICTY, ICTR, Sierra Leone, ICC.[44]
- International Crimes Database (ICD), international crimes adjudicated by national, as well as international and internationalized courts.[45]
- Case Law Database ("CLD") is a gateway to the jurisprudence of the ICTR, ICTY, and IRMCT Appeals Chambers.[46]
- ICC Legal Tools Database is an excellent collection of decisions from international bodies and national courts related to international criminal law. Another tool within this website is the ICC Case Law

42 https://iachr.lls.edu/database.

43 https://www.refworld.org/collections/case-law.

44 https://www.annotatedleadingcases.com/ (subscription database). Also available in print.

45 https://www.internationalcrimesdatabase.org/.

46 https://cld.irmct.org/.

Database. There are many ways to do powerful searching in this database.[47]

- Peter Robinson's Summaries of Decisions (Digests) from the ICC, IRMCT, ICTR, and ICTY.[48]

6.4 DOCKETS AND COURT FILINGS

It is common for American legal researchers to obtain the dockets and court filings for many U.S. federal and state courts. However, access to these kinds of materials for international courts (not to mention non-U.S. courts) is much more challenging. Once again, there is no one-stop shop for this information. If it is available at all, you need to consult the court's website for information about access to these materials and to determine what kinds of official publications are produced by the court. Available dockets (or docket-like information) will vary as well as access to pleadings. For example, the ICJ and ITLOS provide access to pleadings and other documents from the websites as well as in print collections.[49] In some instances, webcasts of oral proceedings are also available from the court, as in the case of ITLOS.[50] Bloomberg Law does provide dockets for the European Court of Justice from

---

[47] https://www.legal-tools.org/ and https://www.legal-tools.org/cld.

[48] https://peterrobinson.com/digests/.

[49] For example, the publications page of the ITLOS website lists the publication containing pleadings, https://www.itlos.org/index.php?id=14&L=0.

[50] https://www.itlos.org/en/main/cases/webcast/.

01/2003 to present; however, there is very limited information available and no access to the actual documents. Documents may be available by request.

6.5 COMMENTARY

When researching international cases, commentary and analysis are useful for several reasons. Journal articles and books are quite helpful when you are trying to identify cases on a specific topic or from a specific court. While most courts and tribunals have websites, their sites may not provide a user-friendly search mechanism or any other tool for locating cases by topic. This is when Lexis and Westlaw can provide more powerful search capabilities, but these databases have limited collections of cases from international courts and tribunals. There is no one-size-fits-all solution in this area.

Commentary and analysis are also useful for obtaining information on the practice and procedure of a specific court. These kinds of materials deal with jurisdiction, the structure and powers of the courts, procedure, evidence, judgments, appeals, and more. Such titles include *Archbold International Criminal Courts: Practice, Procedure and Evidence* (5th ed. 2018), *The Practice and Procedure of the Inter-American Court of Human Rights* (2nd ed. 2013), and *Research Handbook on International Procedural Law* (Joanna Gomula, Stephan Wittich & Markus Stemeseder, eds., 2024). Journal articles can be good sources for information on specific processes in these same courts. A good source for such articles is *The*

Law & Practice of International Courts and Tribunals (2002–)[51] and the *Journal of International Dispute Settlement* (2010–).[52] Both of these journals are indexed in the *Index to Foreign Legal Periodicals* (IFLP).[53]

Finally, books, articles, and research papers are all good for delving into the issues surrounding these bodies. For example, if you are interested in the legal reasoning behind the establishment of Extraordinary African Chambers in the Senegalese Courts (EAC), you would want to read Sara Williams' article called "The Extraordinary African Chambers in the Senegalese Courts: An African Solution to an African Problem?," 11 *J. Int'l Crim. Justice* 1139 (2013). Oxford University Press publishes an "International Courts and Tribunals Series" addressing both legal and policy aspects of the work of these bodies.[54] See Chapter 10 of this *Nutshell* for more information on what tools to use to locate commentary and analysis.

6.6 COURT UPDATES

To stay updated on new jurisprudence, there are a few tools available. If you are interested in monitoring war crimes trials, check out War Crimes

---

[51] Available electronically on Brill Online, https://brill.com/view/journals/lape/lape-overview.xml (subscription database).

[52] Available electronically on Oxford's website, https://academic.oup.com/jids (subscription database).

[53] Available electronically on HeinOnline, https://heinonline.org/ (subscription database).

[54] https://global.oup.com/academic/content/series/i/international-courts-and-tribunals-series-icts/?cc=us&lang=en& (subscription database).

Prosecution Watch, a biweekly electronic newsletter that collects information about documents and news articles on this topic throughout the world.[55] Many international law blogs also report on new decisions and the work of courts and tribunals. Another way to stay up-to-date on new decisions and the activities of courts and tribunals is to subscribe to press releases and updates via email on individual court websites. For example, the International Tribunal for the Law of the Sea allows you to subscribe to press releases and newsletters from the tribunal.[56] Many courts and tribunals also have social media feeds which provide updates on the cases and activities of the court. You may also want to follow international law scholars on social media, such as Beth Van Schaack or Kevin Jon Heller. See Chapter 13 for more information on keeping current.

---

[55] https://www.publicinternationallawandpolicygroup.org/war-crime-watch.

[56] https://www.itlos.org/index.php?id=47&L=0.

CHAPTER 7
EUROPEAN UNION

7.1 INTRODUCTION

Note: The United Kingdom left the European Union on January 21, 2020 (known as "Brexit"). To date, this decision has not impacted research methodology and resources addressed herein.

The European Union (EU) is a unique entity. Born of the dreams of cooperation that sprouted in post-World War II Europe, the EU is comprised of member countries that have surrendered a certain degree of sovereignty in exchange for the economic and political integration then made possible among the States. In theory, the system allows countries to combine their resources, which requires certain political and economic policy decisions affecting Europe to be made collectively. The EU system allows the adoption of common policies involving issues that include agriculture, consumer affairs, culture, the environment, energy, transportation, and trade.

The EU evolved on the premise that collaboration among European nations could put an end to irreconcilable conflicts and generate more efficient beneficial, and amicable decision-making. Though it has its faults, it is important to recognize that the EU represents a real achievement and that it is not meant to create one entity that replaces existing European States. EU member countries maintain a significant amount of sovereignty. Today, the EU's greatest challenge is fostering continued economic and political integration among its members while member countries continue to make independent decisions—and, of course, how to continue and thrive in spite of Brexit.

7.2 THE FORMATION OF THE EU

The origins of European integration can be traced to the series of bloody conflicts between France and Germany from 1870–1945, which some economists and historians have ascribed to a struggle over production of raw materials. In 1950, in the context of a war-weary Europe, French Foreign Minister Robert Schuman urged France and Germany to institute a common Higher Authority to regulate the overall production of coal and steel. It was Schuman who proposed, "the pooling of coal and steel production [to] immediately provide for the setting up of common foundations for economic development and as a first step in the federation of Europe."[1] This idea sparked the creation of the European Coal and Steel Community (ECSC) in 1951, made up of six members: Belgium, West Germany, Luxembourg, France, Italy, and the Netherlands. The High Authority proposed in the Schuman Plan was an independent body charged with making all coal and steel industry decisions involving these countries.

In 1957, after the celebrated success of the ECSC, the original six Member States drafted and signed two treaties that were integral to the formation of the EU. They are known as the "Treaties of Rome." The first of the two treaties was originally called the Treaty Establishing the European Economic

---

[1] Schuman Declaration, May 9, 1950, https://european-union.europa.eu/principles-countries-history/history-eu/1945-59/schuman-declaration-may-1950_en.

Community ("EC Treaty").[2] The second treaty is called the European Atomic Energy Committee (Euratom Treaty).[3] Together, these treaties were intended to remove trade barriers among these member countries and provide guidelines for the formation of a common market. In 1967, the EC replaced its existing institutions with a European Commission, Council of Ministers, and Parliament.

The structural changes in 1967 preface a series of treaties that better define today's EU's structural organization. The 1992 Treaty of Maastricht (formerly the Treaty on European Union) created what is referred to today as the European Union. This treaty set forth a single currency for the EU as well as the EU's three-pillar system. This treaty also introduced new methods of cooperation among the governments of Member States, especially in the areas of defense and home affairs.

The Treaty of Maastricht was further supplemented by the Treaty of Amsterdam in 1997 and the Treaty of Nice in 2001. Both treaties were designed to handle the challenges resulting from the burgeoning membership of the European Union. To ensure that the expanding EU could continue functioning efficiently, a more streamlined system for decision-making was an absolute necessity. The Treaty of Nice introduced new rules governing the size of the EU institutions and the functions they

---

[2] In 1992, the Maastricht Treaty amended the EC Treaty and removed the word "economic" from its title.

[3] All treaties are available at https://eur-lex.europa.eu/collection/eu-law/treaties/treaties-force.html.

serve. If approved by all EU Member States, an official EU Constitution was scheduled for ratification in 2006. However, due to some ratification problems, the EU entered into a "period of reflection," and in June 2007, decided not to pass a constitution. Instead, an Intergovernmental Conference (IGC) was convened to work on drafting a reform treaty, and the Treaty of Lisbon was signed on December 13, 2007.[4] This treaty amends the current EU and EC treaties and entered into force on December 1, 2009.[5]

7.3 THE EU TODAY

The EU's membership now totals 27 countries:[6] Austria, Belgium, Bulgaria, Croatia, Cyprus, the Czech Republic, Denmark, Estonia, Finland, France, Germany, Greece, Hungary, Ireland, Italy, Latvia, Lithuania, Luxembourg, Malta, the Netherlands, Poland, Portugal, Romania, Slovakia, Slovenia, Spain, and Sweden.[7] Other countries wish to join the EU, and admitting new members presents many complications.

---

[4] https://european-union.europa.eu/principles-countries-history/principles-and-values/founding-agreements_en.

[5] *Id.*

[6] https://european-union.europa.eu/principles-countries-history/eu-countries_en.

[7] As noted at the top of this chapter, the UK voted to leave the EU on June 23, 2016. Brexit was accomplished on January 31, 2020. For more information and relevant documents, see https://eur-lex.europa.eu/content/news/Brexit-UK-withdrawal-from-the-eu.html. For more information on researching this issue, see the Bodleian Library Research Guide, "European Union Law: Brexit," https://libguides.bodleian.ox.ac.uk/c.php?g=422926&p=4678442.

7.4 THE EURO[8]

As a symbol of a single European market, the euro represents one of the most significant economic reforms in history and serves as the official currency of the EU. Even non-EU states of Europe, including Monaco and Vatican City, have adopted the euro as their currency. The European System of Central Banks administers the euro and possesses sole authority to set the EU's monetary policy. The United Kingdom never adopted the euro.

7.5 THE EU'S ORGANIZATIONAL STRUCTURE

The governmental structure of the EU is divided among five main institutions that create a system of checks and balances: the European Commission, European Parliament, Council of the European Union, European Council, and the Court of Justice of the European Union.[9] Each of these institutions has a specific role in shaping, implementing, and monitoring EU policy and regulations. The descriptions below are quite brief, so be sure to consult the EU website for a full description of the roles and responsibilities of these institutions.

---

[8] https://european-union.europa.eu/institutions-law-budget/euro_en.

[9] https://european-union.europa.eu/institutions-law-budget/institutions-and-bodies/search-all-eu-institutions-and-bodies_en.

A. THE EUROPEAN COMMISSION[10]

Based in Brussels, the European Commission serves as the executive branch of the EU, managing policies and the annual budget. The Commission is responsible for drafting all legislative and policy proposals for European laws. These proposals are then submitted to the Council and to the European Parliament for amendment and approval.

After consultation with the European Parliament, the President of the Commission is nominated by common agreement among the governments of the Member States. The nomination of the President is accompanied by the nomination of 27 Commissioners. Commissioners are nominated by the governments of each member state according to its own selection procedure. The Parliament must then vote to approve the appointment of the President and the other members of the Commission. If the appointment of any Commissioner is denied by the Parliament, the selection process must start again.

The President of the Commission sets out the EU's political priorities in a multiannual overview called the "work programme." Commissioners are expected to act independently and in the best interest of the EU as a whole. They do not have any individual decision-making powers, except when authorized to

---

10 https://commission.europa.eu/index_en.

take measures in their own name and in their area of responsibility.[11]

B. THE EUROPEAN PARLIAMENT[12]

The European Parliament, a legislative body elected every five years by universal suffrage, monitors the European Commission and oversees the EU budget. Although the Parliament's official headquarters are in Strasbourg, the majority of its committee work and plenary sessions happen in Brussels. The more than 700 members of the European Parliament (MEPs) are not organized by nationality, but by political allegiance. The Parliament has no authority to propose legislation directly, but it may request the European Commission to propose legislation, and it must approve most EU laws (with the Council of the EU).

C. THE EUROPEAN COUNCIL AND THE COUNCIL OF THE EUROPEAN UNION[13]

These are two very closely tied institutions. While the names are similar (causing lots of confusion), they have different roles and membership.

The European Council works on overall political direction and policy for the EU, but it has no role in legislation. Its members are the heads of state of the governments of the 27 EU Member States, the

---

[11] https://commission.europa.eu/about-european-commission_en.

[12] https://www.europarl.europa.eu/portal/en.

[13] https://www.consilium.europa.eu/en/.

European Council President, and the President of the European Commission.[14]

The European Parliament shares its legislative power with the Council of the European Union (also known as the EU Council), the main decision-making body of the EU. Presidency of the Council is held for six months by each member state on rotation. The Council serves as a discussion forum for the government ministers representing EU Member States.[15]

D. COURT OF JUSTICE OF THE EUROPEAN UNION[16]

Sitting in Luxembourg, the European Court of Justice is the judicial organ of the European Community. As discussed in Chapter 6, the Court is divided into two bodies: the Court of Justice and the General Court (which absorbed the Civil Service Tribunal in 2016). Each of the Member States appoints a judge to serve on the Court to ensure that all legal systems of member countries are represented. One of the Court's primary functions is to ensure that EU law is properly applied throughout all of the EU countries. It also settles legal disputes between governments and EU institutions. Under limited circumstances, businesses and individuals can bring an action against an EU institution.

---

[14] https://www.consilium.europa.eu/en/european-council/.

[15] https://european-union.europa.eu/institutions-law-budget/institutions-and-bodies/search-all-eu-institutions-and-bodies/council-european-union_en.

[16] https://curia.europa.eu/jcms/jcms/j_6/en/.

In addition to 27 judges, there are 11 Advocates General. The Advocates General assist the Court and write impartial opinions in their areas of specialized expertise.

E. ADDITIONAL EU BODIES[17]

There are additional entities that work in collaboration with the five main institutions of the EU: the Court of Auditors, the European Economic and Social Committee, the Committee of the Regions, the European Central Bank, the European Ombudsman, and the European Investment Bank.

Also based in Luxembourg, the Court of Auditors was set up in 1975 as an ancillary body for monitoring the EU budget. The Court consists of one member from each country belonging to the EU, appointed by the Council for a renewable term of six years. The Court's primary role is to make sure "EU funds are collected and used correctly and help improve EU financial management."[18]

The European Economic and Social Committee (EESC) is an advisory body representing employers, trade unions, farmers, consumers, and other interest groups. The EESC serves as a representative for these interest groups and presents their concerns

---

[17] https://european-union.europa.eu/institutions-law-budget/institutions-and-bodies/search-all-eu-institutions-and-bodies_en.

[18] https://european-union.europa.eu/institutions-law-budget/institutions-and-bodies/search-all-eu-institutions-and-bodies/european-court-auditors-eca_en.

during policy discussions with the Commission, the Council, and the European Parliament.[19]

The Committee of the Regions (CoR) is comprised of representatives of Europe's regional and local authorities.[20] According to the Treaty on European Union, the CoR must be consulted before the EU can make decisions on matters that concern local and regional governments.[21]

Also set up under the Treaty of the European Union, the European Central Bank is responsible for instituting the EU's monetary policy and managing the euro.[22]

The European Investment Bank (EIB) was created under the Treaty of Rome. As a non-profit entity, the EIB uses separate funds from the EU budget to invest in countries that are candidates for EU membership, in small businesses, and in developing nations.[23]

---

19 https://european-union.europa.eu/institutions-law-budget/institutions-and-bodies/search-all-eu-institutions-and-bodies/european-economic-and-social-committee-eesc_en.

20 https://european-union.europa.eu/institutions-law-budget/institutions-and-bodies/search-all-eu-institutions-and-bodies/european-committee-regions-cor_en.

21 Treaty on European Union, Feb. 7, 1992, 1992 O.J. (C191) 1, 31 I.L.M. 253 (1992).

22 https://european-union.europa.eu/institutions-law-budget/institutions-and-bodies/search-all-eu-institutions-and-bodies/european-central-bank-ecb_en.

23 https://european-union.europa.eu/institutions-law-budget/institutions-and-bodies/search-all-eu-institutions-and-bodies/european-investment-bank-eib_en.

The European Ombudsman is elected for a five-year term and serves as an intermediary between citizens and EU authorities. When citizens, businesses, organizations, and those with a registered office in an EU country want to file grievances, it is the Ombudsman who receives them and investigates.[24]

For more information on these and other institutions and bodies, see the website called "Your Gateway to the European Union (formerly called EUROPA website).[25]

7.6 EUROPEAN UNION DOCUMENTS

The EU document system is as massive as the UN system. But there is good news—the EU has taken full advantage of the web as the primary mechanism for distributing documents. Before going straight to the computer to search for documents, an overview of the documentation available from EU bodies and institutions is in order.

For most researchers, the Gateway site,[26] the official website of the European Union, is the best place to start since it provides a tremendous amount of the most important documentation and information. This website provides basic information on the EU, news and events, and links to the sites of

---

[24] https://european-union.europa.eu/institutions-law-budget/institutions-and-bodies/search-all-eu-institutions-and-bodies/european-ombudsman_en.

[25] https://european-union.europa.eu/institutions-law-budget/institutions-and-bodies/search-all-eu-institutions-and-bodies_en.

[26] https://european-union.europa.eu/index_en.

all the EU institutions and bodies. Information on this site is available in all the twenty-four official languages of the EU (plus Russian and Ukrainian), and there is no charge to access any of the documents.

Of particular importance to the legal researcher is EUR-Lex.[27] This should be the first database consulted since it contains a variety of law and law-related documents: treaties, international agreements, legislation in force, legislation in preparation, case law, and parliamentary questions. Like other parts of EUROPA, access to this collection of documents is also free.

Be aware of "eurojargon" when using EU materials. Sometimes you may need to consult a glossary for help with definitions of unfamiliar terminology. To this end, the European Parliament has a Technology Coordination Unit, and they provide several tools for deciphering EU terminology, like glossaries and the database called IATE (InterActive Terminology for Europe).[28]

7.7 SOME BASICS FOR DOING EU LEGAL RESEARCH

The *Official Journal of the European Union* (often cited to as OJ) is divided into two series: the *L Series* and the *C Series*. The *L Series* contains adopted treaties and legislation, including directives and regulations, adopted by the Commission and Council, and other founding acts. The *C Series* is the

---

[27] https://eur-lex.europa.eu/homepage.html.

[28] https://iate.europa.eu/home.

"Information and Notices" section of the OJ containing the following: non-binding decisions and resolutions of the institutions; texts of proposed legislation; minutes of the Parliament; Commission and Council replies to written questions; opinions of the Economic and Social Committee; and notices of Court decisions. Two subseries, LI and CI, were introduced in 2016 to allow for more flexibility in case of unplanned content changes.[29] The EUR-Lex website contains electronic copies of all of the OJs since the first edition.[30] Electronic editions of the OJ (e–OJ) published after July 1, 2013, are "authentic and shall produce legal effects"[31] and contain an advanced electronic signature guaranteeing authenticity. The paper version no longer has legal value.[32]

7.8 LEGISLATION

A. EUROPEAN UNION TREATIES

The basic legal texts upon which the European Union and the European Communities are based are the treaties: the founding treaties, plus amendments; the accession treaties for each of the five enlargements; and other important treaties and

---

29 https://eur-lex.europa.eu/content/help/oj/series-and-subseries.html.

30 https://eur-lex.europa.eu/oj/direct-access.html.

31 See Regulation (EU) No 216/2013, https://eur-lex.europa.eu/legal-content/EN/TXT/?uri=CELEX:32013R0216.

32 https://eur-lex.europa.eu/content/help/oj/authenticity-eOJ.html.

protocols.[33] EUR-Lex provides the text in html, pdf from the OJ, and with an e-signature. Treaties are also available in print and on Lexis, Westlaw, and other websites.

Primary legislation includes the founding (or constitutive) treaties from the ESCS Treaty of 1957 to the Treaty of Lisbon of 2007. A second source of primary law consists of the treaties between Member States and treaties between the EU and third parties.

B. SECONDARY LEGISLATION

The major source of Community legislation is secondary legislation: regulations, directives, decisions, and other non-binding recommendations and opinions. A few definitions are in order.

- Regulations are laws adopted by the Council of the European Union upon a proposal from the Commission. Regulations have general effect and are directly applicable in all the Member States. Regulations do not require national implementing legislation.
- Directives are laws adopted by the Council of the European Union upon a proposal from the Commission. Directives are addressed to the Member States and are binding as to the result—Member States may choose the form

---

[33] https://eur-lex.europa.eu/collection/eu-law/treaties/treaties-force.html.

and methods of implementation. The process of implementation is called harmonization.

- Decisions are laws, issued by the Council or Commission, which are binding on those addressed, whether they be governments, companies, or individuals.
- Opinions are written statements by the Council or Commission and have no binding force. Opinions are an important indication of Council or Commission policy.
- Recommendations adopted by the Commission are like directives in that they are applicable only on the Member States cited and only with respect to the end result. They have no binding force.

7.9 DOCUMENTATION OF EU INSTITUTIONS

Each EU institution (outlined in section 7.5) generates specific documents and reports. The aim here is to focus on the documents of most interest to a legal researcher. For access and explanation of other documents, see the specific website of the institution or body of interest or use search tool on EUROPA website.

One of the most important institutions in the legal area is the European Commission[34] because it has both executive and administrative roles. The Commission is organized into departments, called

---

[34] https://commission.europa.eu/index_en.

Directorates-General, which are responsible for drafting legislation and overseeing its implementation. In its executive capacity, the Commission acts as the "government" in a Parliamentary system by initiating legislation and submitting proposals to the Council of the European Union. The Commission also oversees Member States' implementation of directives and enforces regulations.

Commission documents (also known as "COM documents") are good for explanatory memoranda and the text of proposed legislation. The Commission also produces Green and White Papers and SEC documents. Green papers are discussion papers on a specific policy area. White papers are documents containing proposals for Community action in a specific area. SEC documents are internal documents associated with the decision-making process and the general operation of Commission departments. Commission documents are accessible on EUR-Lex.[35] To promote transparency, the Commission's website has information on ways to access documents as well as historical archives.[36]

The Parliament, the Council of the European Union, and the European Commission are the main

---

[35] https://eur-lex.europa.eu/browse/institutions/eu-commission.html.

[36] https://commission.europa.eu/about-european-commission/service-standards-and-principles/transparency/access-documents_en.

decision-making bodies of the EU.[37] The EU Council represents the Member States, acts on Commission proposals, and has final legislative authority. The Council may request that certain legislation be proposed and may conduct any necessary studies to help achieve the goals of foundational treaties. The Council also has treaty-making power.

The Council issues working papers on legislation, minutes, and other documents. See the "Documents & Publications"[38] section of the website for access (through what is called the "public register'). The site also provides a database of treaties and agreements,[39] which includes agreements with non-EU countries as well as other international organizations. If the treaty has been published in the Official Journal, a link to the OJ will be available from this database. The search mechanism available for this database is quite limited, so use the "list of parties" instead.

The European Parliament[40] is composed of Representatives directly elected by the populations of EU Member States. In most cases, the Council is required to submit proposed legislation to the European Parliament for comment. The Parliament acts as a forum for debate and for the questioning of

---

[37] https://european-union.europa.eu/institutions-law-budget/law/how-eu-policy-decided_en.

[38] https://www.consilium.europa.eu/en/documents-publications/.

[39] https://www.consilium.europa.eu/en/documents-publications/treaties-agreements/.

[40] https://www.europarl.europa.eu/portal/en.

the Council and Commission. The appropriate committee of the Parliament scrutinizes the proposed legislation, and a rapporteur is selected to draft a report and opinion for consideration at the plenary meeting. Most legislation is adopted using the ordinary legislative procedure (formerly known as "codecision"), whereby both the Parliament and the Council adopt the legislative proposal.[41]

For first or second readings of Commission proposals, see Reports, which generally consists of three parts: 1) a record of the Committee's action; 2) an explanatory memorandum providing background on an issue and reasons for the Committee's recommendation; and 3) the text of the draft opinion. Minutes of plenary sessions considering the rapporteur's report are printed in the C series of the OJ. The Parliament's website contains a "Documents" section where you can search for these materials by Committee or keyword. Debates of the plenary sessions of Parliament and videos of speeches are also available.[42]

The European Economic and Social Committee[43] is an advisory body representing workers' and employers' organizations and other interest groups. This Committee is composed of members appointed by the Member States. During the legislative process, the Council of Ministers may be required to decide (or

---

41 https://www.europarl.europa.eu/about-parliament/en/powers-and-procedures/legislative-powers.

42 http://www.europarl.europa.eu/plenary/en/debates-video.html.

43 https://www.eesc.europa.eu/en.

may do so on its own initiative) to seek the opinion of the Committee.

Documents and texts from the Economic and Social Committee are available on the Committee's website.

The European Court of Justice[44] is the highest legal authority in the EU. The Court is empowered to decide cases involving interpretation and application of the EU law. EU institutions and Member States may appeal and take each other to court for failure to implement or properly apply the Treaties and derived legislation (for example, the Commission will file a case against a Member State for not implementing a directive). A legal or natural person may appeal to the Court against a decision addressed to her or any regulation or decision which is of direct concern to her. The Court will also issue prejudicial decisions in cases referred to it by national courts when questions of EU law are involved. The Advocate-generals present a reasoned and independent opinion of the issue of law in the case. While there is no formal doctrine of stare decisis, the Court tends to follow its own decisions. The decisions are binding on the national courts of Member States.

The General Court has jurisdiction to hear and determine at first instance all types of action not under the jurisdiction of the Court of Justice—in particular, actions brought by individuals. In practice, this means that the General Court deals

---

[44] https://curia.europa.eu/jcms/.

mainly with competition law, State aid, trade, agriculture, and trademarks.

The judgments from both courts are available in the official *European Court Reports* series (ECR),[45] the Court's website, Lexis, and Westlaw.

7.10 FINDING DIRECTIVES AND REGULATIONS

All directives and regulations are published in the L series of the OJ, and EUR-Lex is the best place to obtain legislation. If you have the OJ citation, use EUR-Lex as noted below. Otherwise, there is a more advanced search tool on the site.

Before jumping over to EUR-Lex, you should be aware of the different numbering systems for legislation.

Numbering before 1/1/2015:

- (EC) 408/98 (regulation)
- 93/13 (EC) (directive)
- OJ citation
    - 1993 OJ L 95/29
        - L 95 is the issue number, 29 is the page number

---

45 The paper version of the ECR ceased in 2009 and since January 1, 2012, the Reports are available exclusively in digital format on the EUR-Lex and Curia websites, see https://curia.europa.eu/jcms/jcms/P_101083/en/.

New numbering system: harmonizing EU law numbering after 1/1/15:

- (domain) Year/Number
  - Regulation (EU) 2015/1
  - Directive (EU) 2015/2

Domain indicates the type of document (regulation or directive), then the year and the document number: Council Regulation (EU) 2015/373, 2015 OJ L 64/6.

If you have the OJ citations, as noted above, you can go directly to the Official Journal and get what you need. The OJ is available on EUR-Lex, print, Lexis, and Westlaw (as well as a few other databases, like vLex). If you only have the numbers for the EU legislation and not a clue where to go, start with EUR-Lex. For example, search 2002/58 on EUR-Lex, by using the document number; type in the year (2002) and number (38) in the appropriate boxes. Since you don't know the type of document, you will retrieve fifteen relevant results. If you are looking for legislation, you can filter your search to "legal acts" and that reduces your results to seven documents. Four of these documents are "corrigendum" (a document used to correct errors in the language of a legal act), so that leaves three relevant documents and two of them are most likely what you need—a regulation or a directive.

One the most useful aspects of EUR-Lex is the "Document Information" linked from each item on the results list. This document information is a very important research tool. From here, you can get the text of the legislation; learn about the proper classifications (using Euro-jargon); get a COM document number (the Commission's proposal for the legislation); find the legal basis from the founding treaties, amendments, and citations to case law from the European Court of Justice; and more—all for free!

Of course, you won't always have a citation to the piece of legislation. Say you need a directive on the conduct of clinical trials on medicine for human use. Using the advanced search mechanism, search the "Text search" field using the terms "human use" and "clinical trials." You can limit this search to the title or the text. By limiting the search to the title, this search retrieves one result. You can also utilize the detailed "document information" as mentioned above or go directly to the document.

Due to the complexities of the EU language, you may find searching for legislation using Lexis or Westlaw more satisfying. Both databases offer better search flexibility than EUR-Lex.

Another option for locating relevant legislation is to use the directories. Directories allow you to access EU law by subject, but you must be aware of the EU classification scheme in order to use this tool effectively. To locate regulations and directives, use the Directory of European Union Legislation[46] or the Directory of European Union Preparatory Acts.[47]

7.11 IMPLEMENTING LEGISLATION

Member States must pass national legislation to implement EU directives. Locating implementing legislation is not as easy as locating the EU directive. The EUR-Lex record has a section called "National Transposition" and this provides the implementation measures communicated by the Member States. While no legislation is linked to the record, at least you have information necessary to locate the text of the document: the name of the law, the law number, and the date of the law. Note that this information may not contain any subsequent amendments to the original implementing legislation.

Westlaw also provides references to national legislation by Member States at the end of documents under the heading "national measures," usually in the language of the country.

A website called N-Lex ("a common gateway to national law") is available from the EU.[48] This site does not provide access to national law, but it does allow you to search national legislative databases in a standard way, more or less. The laws are not translated into English, unless English is one of the

---

46 https://eur-lex.europa.eu/browse/directories/legislation.html.

47 https://eur-lex.europa.eu/browse/directories/legislation-preparation.html.

48 https://n-lex.europa.eu/n-lex/index?lang=en.

official languages of that country. There is a general introduction to the legislative database for each country, and this is often in English. By consulting the "national implementing measures" section of EUR-Lex, you can identify the needed legislation and then use N-Lex to obtain the law.

The EUR-Lex website also provides search tools for locating national legislation (national transposition).[49] The most efficient way to search is to use the "national transposition measures for legal acts" section and search by the directive year and number.

Another handy source for obtaining citations to relevant national legislation is *European Current Law: Monthly Digest* (1992–) and the *European Current Law Year Book* (1993–). With these sources, you can research laws by EU legislation, subject, or country. You can then use the databases noted in N-Lex or research guides to locate the relevant law.

See Chapter 3 of this *Nutshell* for help with researching foreign law.

7.12 CASE LAW

There are many tools available for locating the jurisprudence of the European Court of Justice. Using EUR-Lex, select "EU case law" from the "EU law and related documents" tab.[50] You can also use the Directory of European Union case law to browse

---

[49] https://eur-lex.europa.eu/collection/n-law/mne.html.

[50] https://eur-lex.europa.eu/collection/eu-law/eu-case-law.html.

by EU classification scheme to locate judgments. In addition, the Court has its own website called Curia.[51] On this site, you can search by completing a search form, browsing a numerical list, or using a digest and alphabetical list—if you can read French. The search form (under "Case-Law")[52] is usually the best place to start, especially if you know the case number, the parties, or have a reference to another case or legislation.

There are three commercial databases that provide access to cases: Lexis, Westlaw, and vLex.[53] The advantage of using these databases is the ability to search the entire text and to use advanced search techniques.

To locate national court decisions on EU law, see the National Decisions database, containing references to decisions from 1959 to present.[54] Another similar database is available on EUR-Lex.[55] As noted above, *European Current Law: Monthly Digest* (1992–) and the *European Current Law Year Book* (1993–) can also be useful for locating relevant decisions. All of these resources may require locating the cases using national court websites or other databases.

---

[51] https://curia.europa.eu/jcms/jcms/j_6/en/.

[52] https://curia.europa.eu/juris/recherche.jsf?language=en.

[53] See Appendix A.

[54] https://www.aca-europe.eu/index.php/en/dec-nat-en.

[55] https://eur-lex.europa.eu/collection/n-law/n-case-law.html.

7.13 BACKGROUND SOURCES

Launching into an analysis of European Union law through legislation can be overwhelming. Since there are many good books published on the EU and on any number of topics, a quick review of these sources is worth the time. Keep in mind that many of these titles will not cover Brexit and related issues, but they do cover the fundamentals of EU law.

Encyclopedia of European Union Law (1996–).

European Union Law Guide (2011–).[56]

The Evolution of EU Law (Paul Craig & Gráinne de Búrca, eds., 3rd ed. 2021).

Ralph Folsom, *European Union Law including Brexit and Beyond in a Nutshell* (10th ed. 2021).

Nigel Foster, *Foster on EU Law* (8th ed. 2021).

Oxford Encyclopedia of EU Law (OEEUL) (2023–).[57]

Oxford Principles of European Union Law (Professor Robert Schütze & Professor Takis Tridimas, eds., 2018).

Smit & Herzog on the Law of the European Union (2nd ed. 2010–).[58]

---

[56] Also available on Westlaw.

[57] Available on Oxford Public International Law, https://opil.ouplaw.com/home/OEEUL (subscription database).

[58] Also available on Lexis.

Takis Tridimas, *The Foundations of European Union Law* (9th ed. 2024).

There are also many journal articles on the EU in the legal literature. Use the tools noted in Chapter 10 for more assistance. *Legal Journals Index* (LJI) is particularly useful for locating articles on EU law.[59]

7.14 OTHER USEFUL TOOLS

There are many other tools and guides on the web to help research this vast area of law. Here is a short list of some good resources:

- European e-Justice Portal.[60] Information on national justice systems throughout the EU, see the "Legislation and case law" section.
- European Union—A Guide to Tracing Working Documents.[61]
- European Union Legal Materials: An Infrequent User's Guide.[62]
- IATE ("Inter-Active Terminology for Europe").[63] EU's inter-institutional terminology database.

---

59 Available electronically on Westlaw.

60 https://e-justice.europa.eu/home.do?action=home&plang=en.

61 https://www.nyulawglobal.org/globalex/European_Union_Travaux_Preparatoires1.html.

62 https://www.nyulawglobal.org/globalex/European_Union1.html.

63 https://iate.europa.eu/home.

- European Law Blog: News and Comments on EU Law.[64]

[64] https://europeanlawblog.eu/.

CHAPTER 8
UNITED NATIONS

8.1 INTRODUCTION

There is a wide range of misconceptions regarding the structure and purpose of the world's largest and most inclusive global organization—the UN. Some think that it functions as a world government policing international affairs, some that it is a mere, toothless bureaucracy devoid of meaningful influence. A more apt description, however, is that the UN plays an important, though evolving, diplomatic role in an increasingly complex global setting. Although the UN is not a world government, and it does not pass laws in the traditional sense, it does provide a framework and forum for resolving international conflicts and developing foreign policy. As such, it generates a veritable avalanche of documents in every possible format. An overview of the UN's formation and a summary of its six primary bodies offer a basic understanding of the UN's role in international affairs. It will assist researchers in battling the most common misconceptions and, perhaps, make research that touches on UN materials a bit less mysterious.

8.2 THE LEAGUE OF NATIONS: PREDECESSOR TO THE UN

While the history of international efforts to create a global peacekeeping body is quite vast, the seminal event is the founding of the League of Nations following the end of the First World War. As part of an agreement between Germany and the Allies to end the global conflict, the League of Nations was established under the Treaty of Versailles "to promote international cooperation and to achieve peace and security."[1] The League of Nations was an association of states that pledged not to go to war before submitting their disputes to formal arbitration or inquiry. This mechanism was designed to prevent acts of unilateral aggression and to promote a more stable geopolitical system.

The League of Nations formally came into existence on January 10, 1920. Autonomous, but closely connected to the League of Nations, were the Permanent Court of International Justice and the International Labor Organization. The League also established subsidiary bodies to promote cooperation on economic, social, health, and intellectual matters. Lacking formal support and participation from the United States, the League of Nations never achieved strong influence globally. After failing to prevent the Second World War, the League ceased its activities. When the Second World War ended, a renewed global desire for peace prompted calls for a similar organization to carry the torch—the result was the UN.

This chapter will not cover researching the documents issued by the League of Nations (except for treaties). If you need to locate such documents, see Gabriela Femenia, "Researching League of Nations Documents" (2024).[2]

---

1 The Versailles Treaty, June 28, 1919, https://avalon.law.yale.edu/subject_menus/versailles_menu.asp.

2 https://www.nyulawglobal.org/globalex/league_nations_guide1.html.

8.3 THE FORMATION OF THE UN

The need for an international organization to replace the League of Nations was first acknowledged during World War II, in the Moscow Declaration issued by China, Great Britain, the U.S., and the USSR on October 30, 1943.[3] Following the end of the war in 1945, representatives of 50 nations attended the founding conference in San Francisco, where they drafted and later signed the UN Charter.[4] The required 29 nations ratified the Charter on October 26, 1945, making the organization official.

The current membership of the UN totals 193 countries. Agreement and acceptance of the obligations put forth in the UN Charter are required for a state to become a member of the UN. A defining feature of UN membership remains the fact that Member States relinquish none of their sovereignty in exchange for membership. The Charter is designed as an international treaty outlining the basic principles of international relations. According to the Charter, the UN has four purposes: (1) to maintain international peace and security; (2) to develop friendly relations among nations; (3) to cooperate in solving international problems and in promoting

---

[3] In addition to proposing the need for an international organization for peace, the Moscow Declaration demanded the unconditional surrender of the Axis powers and declared Germany's annexation of Austria illegal.

[4] L.M. Goodrich et al., *Charter of the United Nations: Commentary and Documents* (3rd ed. 1969).

respect for human rights; and (4) to be a center for harmonizing the actions of nations.[5]

8.4 A ROADMAP: THE ORGANIZATIONAL STRUCTURE OF THE UN

Like any complex political system, the UN consists of several branches that have specific powers and responsibilities. In fact, given its organization and its name, it is no surprise that the UN has been confused for a world government. Of its six main entities, five of them are based at the UN Headquarters in New York City: the Security Council, the Secretariat, the General Assembly, the Economic and Social Council, and the Trusteeship Council. The sixth, the International Court of Justice, is located at The Hague in the Netherlands.

A. THE SECURITY COUNCIL[6]

The Security Council's primary role is to lead UN decision-making with regard to threats against international peace and acts of aggression.[7] The Council also acts as part of the broader UN leadership in advising the decision-making of the General Assembly in such matters as choosing a new Secretary General or admitting new Member States. Under the UN Charter, all members are obligated to abide by the Council's decisions.

---

[5] UN Charter, art. 1, paras. 1–4, https://www.un.org/en/about-us/un-charter.

[6] https://www.un.org/securitycouncil/.

[7] UN Charter, ch. VII, art. 39, https://www.un.org/en/about-us/un-charter.

Of the 15 Council members, five nations have permanent seats: China, France, the Russian Federation, the United Kingdom, and the United States. The other 10 are elected by the General Assembly for two-year terms. Nine affirmative votes are required for the Council to make a decision. Each of the five permanent members has veto power. This means that any one of the five permanent members can stop any decision. The only exception to this rule is when procedural matters are under consideration.[8]

The Security Council may meet at any time. If the Council determines a situation to be a potential threat to international peace, it will convene and initiate an attempt to mediate and resolve the conflict peacefully. If a conflict has already resulted in an attack, the Council will make haste towards a ceasefire. The Council has authority to assign peacekeeping missions in those situations where parties require more assistance in maintaining truces or where a physical separation of opposing forces is imperative. These are often matters of great political sensitivity.

The Security Council is unique among the UN bodies in that it can impose coercive measures for enforcing its decisions. Enforcement measures include the imposition of economic sanctions and orders for arms embargos.[9] Under extreme circumstances, the Council has authorized Member

---

8 United Nations Security Council, Voting System, https://www.un.org/securitycouncil/content/voting-system.

9 UN Charter, arts. 40–42, https://www.un.org/en/about-us/un-charter.

States to use "all necessary means," including the use of military force. For example, the Council used this authority to give Member States the green light to invade Iraq during the Gulf War in 1990.[10]

B. THE SECRETARIAT[11]

The substantive and administrative work of the UN is managed by the Secretariat under the direction of the General Assembly, the Security Council, and other UN entities. The Secretariat is headed by the Secretary-General[12] and currently requires a global staff of tens of thousands that operate under both the general budget and special funding. Staff members work in duty stations that range from UN Headquarters in New York City to UN offices abroad, including Geneva, Vienna, and Nairobi.[13]

---

[10] S.C. Res. 687, UN Doc. S/RES/687 (1991). In March 1991, Operation Desert Storm ended, and the parties signed a ceasefire agreement. Saddam Hussein consented to United Nations Security Council Resolution 687. The resolution required Iraq to end its weapons of mass destruction programs, recognize the sovereignty of Kuwait, account for missing Kuwaitis, return Kuwaiti property, and end support for international terrorism.

[11] https://www.un.org/en/about-us/secretariat.

[12] https://www.un.org/sg/en/content/sg/biography.

[13] *Composition of the Secretariat: Staff Demographics, Report of the Secretary-General*, UN Doc. A/78/569 (2023), https://digitallibrary.un.org/record/4037810?ln=en&v=pdf. This report is issued annually.

C. THE GENERAL ASSEMBLY[14]

All UN Member States are represented in the General Assembly, a "parliament of nations," which meets to grapple with the world's most pressing problems. All Member States share equal participation, and each is allowed one vote. A two-thirds majority is required for all decisions that involve international peace and security, the admitting of new members, and matters concerning the UN budget. A simple majority is sufficient for all other matters. In recent years, the UN has been trying to reach decisions through consensus, rather than by taking a formal vote.[15]

D. THE ECONOMIC AND SOCIAL COUNCIL[16]

The Economic and Social Council (ECOSOC) is under the jurisdiction of the General Assembly and coordinates the economic and social work of the UN system. The Council consists of 54 members, elected by the General Assembly for three-year terms.[17] Under the UN Charter, the Council has authority to select its own rules of procedure and elect its president.[18] ECOSOC is responsible for over 70% of the human and financial resources of the entire UN

---

[14] https://www.un.org/en/ga/.

[15] https://ask.un.org/faq/260981.

[16] https://ecosoc.un.org/en.

[17] UN Charter, ch. X, art. 61, https://www.un.org/en/about-us/un-charter.

[18] UN Charter, ch. X, art. 72, https://www.un.org/en/about-us/un-charter.

system. The UN is an ocean of acronyms. As you work with them, you'll learn to swim.

In relation to the structure of the UN, ECOSOC serves as a forum for discussing international economic and social issues and for formulating policy recommendations. ECOSOC can invite any member of the UN to participate, without vote, in its deliberations on any matter of particular concern to that state.[19]

ECOSOC oversees the work of the 14 UN specialized agencies, functional commissions, and regional commissions. The five regional commissions are responsible for promoting economic development and cooperation in their respective regions. Other commissions reporting to ECOSOC focus on issues including social development, the status of women, crime prevention, narcotic drugs, and environmental protection. It has the power to make or initiate studies and report on these issues. It also has the power to assist in the preparation and organization of major international conferences in the economic, social, and related fields and to coordinate follow-up to these conferences.

E. THE TRUSTEESHIP COUNCIL[20]

The Trusteeship Council was established under the UN Charter to oversee the preparation of the

---

[19] UN Charter, ch. X, art. 69, https://www.un.org/en/about-us/un-charter.

[20] https://www.un.org/en/about-us/trusteeship-council.

Trust Territories[21] for either self-government or independence. By 1994, the Territories achieved this status, either as separate States or by joining neighboring independent countries. The Trusteeship Council's work culminated in 1994 with the independence of Palau. The Council currently consists of the five permanent members of the Security Council and only schedules meetings by its own decision or at the request of a majority of its members, the General Assembly, or the Security Council.

F. SPECIALIZED AGENCIES AND OTHER PROGRAMS[22]

There are many specialized agencies worldwide that work in concert with the UN. For instance, the International Monetary Fund, World Bank, World Health Organization, and 11 other independent organizations collaborate with UN through cooperative agreements. These organizations were developed by intergovernmental agreement and function autonomously. Together, they cover a comprehensive range of international issues including culture, economics, health, and education.

There are additional, easily recognizable, UN offices, programs, and funds, including the UN Children's Fund (UNICEF); Office of the UN High

---

[21] "Trust Territory," in *Parry & Grant Encyclopaedic Dictionary of International Law* (2009). Available on Oxford Reference, https://www.oxfordreference.com/ (subscription database).

[22] https://www.un.org/en/about-us/un-system.

Commissioner for Refugees (UNHCR); and the UN Development Program (UNDP). Each of these entities reports to either the General Assembly or to ECOSOC. While each has its own governing bodies, budgets, and secretariats, they all work in collaboration with the UN as a whole. Depending on the role of the UN agency, the policies issued may be binding on members as formal international law or may serve as policy recommendations for the construction of binding international law.

G. THE INTERNATIONAL COURT OF JUSTICE[23]

The International Court of Justice (ICJ), sometimes referred to as the World Court, serves as a tribunal to the UN. In addition to providing advisory opinions[24] to the General Assembly and the Security Council, the Court primarily serves as a venue for legal disputes submitted by States. The General Assembly and the Security Council jointly elect fifteen judges to sit on the bench for terms of nine years. The Court may not include more than one judge from any one country. There is no mandate under the UN Charter requiring member States to appear before the Court. However, once they accede or give consent to do so, countries must abide by the Court's decisions.[25] Recognizing that the Court's jurisdiction is voluntary is crucial to comprehending

---

[23] https://www.icj-cij.org/home.

[24] UN Charter, ch. XIV, art. 96, para. 1, https://www.un.org/en/about-us/un-charter.

[25] UN Charter, ch. XIV, art. 94, https://www.un.org/en/about-us/un-charter.

the role of the Court. Even States that are not members of the UN may be brought in as parties if approved by the General Assembly and Security Council.[26] If the Court does not include a judge from a State that is a party to a case, that State may appoint a person to sit as a judge ad hoc for the purpose of the case.

8.5 THE UN'S IMPACT ON HUMAN RIGHTS LAW

In addition to adopting the UN Charter in 1948, the General Assembly also enacted the Universal Declaration of Human Rights (UDHR). The UDHR is used today as a charter of the Human Rights Movement. The UDHR recognizes every individual's right to life, liberty, and personal security without distinction by "race, colour, sex, language, religion, political or other opinion, national or social origin, property, birth or other status."[27] The Declaration has been a powerful tool for the General Assembly in implementing standards for protecting the rights of women, children, disabled persons, minorities, migrant workers, and other vulnerable groups against discriminatory practices. Although the UDHR doesn't have the binding authority to influence State behavior that the UN Charter does, it has gained acceptance as the standard-bearer of

---

[26] UN Charter, ch. XIV, art. 93, para. 2, https://www.un.org/en/about-us/un-charter/.

[27] Universal Declaration of Human Rights, art. 2 and art. 3, https://www.un.org/en/about-us/universal-declaration-of-human-rights.

international human rights norms—or the customary international law of human rights.

8.6 THE UN'S IMPACT ON INTERNATIONAL LAW

The efforts of the UN to promote social and economic development have evolved into an international body of law through conventions, treaties, and standards. The treaties have been used widely to create laws governing international relations. Furthermore, the UN has sponsored over 560 multilateral agreements that are legally binding when ratified by individual countries. Among the issues addressed by these agreements are protecting the environment; regulating migrant labor; curbing drug trafficking; and combating terrorism.

The UN has had difficulty preventing conflicts around the world. An optimist can point with pride to those instances where UN intervention has helped; a pessimist can look to the continuing conflicts and horrors that can be found in the world. UN Member States hold the keys to the organization's success, especially those permanent members of the Security Council, which wield great practical power.

Conflicts aside, it is important to note that in collaboration with other agencies, the UN has seen substantial success as a catalyst for social and economic development around the world. The UN has also promoted normative standards, such as encouraging lawful interactions among all countries. The mechanisms are in place; it is up to the nations of the world to use them.

8.7 UN DOCUMENTS AND PUBLICATIONS

Researching UN documents used to require a trip to a library and digging an enormous collection of paper or microfiche documents. Today's researcher can obtain most UN documents on the web at no cost. Keep in mind that you may still need to use a print or microfiche collection for some older or more obscure documents. These collections will be reviewed at the end of this section.

UN documents are defined as follows: "[a] document is a text submitted to a principal organ or a subsidiary organ of the United Nations for consideration by it, usually in connection with item(s) on its agenda."[28]

The UN documentation system is a massive enterprise, and the legal researcher will never touch many of the documents issued by the UN An excellent overview of the legal materials issued by the UN is contained in the research guide "UN International Law Documentation."[29] This guide "defines the principal UN bodies working in the area of international law; identifies the document series symbols attached to their working documents, as well as the major types of documents and publications they produce; and gives some basic tips for conducting topical searches in the Library's online databases."[30] The principal legal bodies of the UN are

---

[28] https://research.un.org/en/docs.

[29] https://research.un.org/en/docs/law.

[30] See Maureen Ratynski Andersen, "Where to Begin . . . When You Don't Know How to Start: Tips for Researching U.N.

the Sixth Committee of the General Assembly, the International Law Commission, and the United Nations Commission on International Trade Law (UNCITRAL). See the "About UN Documents"[31] for an overview of the documents and publications issued by the principal bodies of the UN.

A. GETTING STARTED

To better understand how UN documents are numbered and organized, it is good to have at least a basic understanding of the structure of the organization. Hopefully, you have read the introduction to the UN at the beginning of this Chapter. To supplement this outline, you should also consult the "About UN Documents."[32] One of the first things this guide does is explain document symbols. Each UN document has its own unique symbol, like an address, and this address is needed for both locating the document in a collection (in any format) and is also useful for citation purposes. As stated in the research guide: "Symbols include both letters and numbers. Some elements of the symbol have meaning, while other elements do not. In general, the symbol does not indicate the topic of the document."[33]

It is important to note that the symbol remains the same no matter the language of the document. So, if you find a document in Spanish and need it in

---

Legal Materials," 31 *Int'l J. Legal Info.* 264 (2003). Available on HeinOnline (subscription database).

[31] https://research.un.org/en/docs.

[32] https://research.un.org/en/docs.

[33] https://research.un.org/en/docs/symbols.

English, the symbol on the Spanish version can be used to locate the English-language document.

The first component of the symbol is the abbreviation for the parent organ or body. The second element indicates the subsidiary body. Special components indicate the nature of the document, and the final component indicates if there have been modifications.

For example, A/CONF.157/PC/63/Add.4

A/:	General Assembly
CONF.157/:	World Conference on Human Rights
PC/:	Preparatory Committee
63/:	Document number 63
Add.4:	Addendum 4

The research guide mentioned above provides greater detail on UN document symbols and should be consulted when trying to decipher an unfamiliar document symbol.

There are other document numbers to be aware of when using UN documents. Some documents have "sales numbers." These are usually publications that are of general interest. Some publications might have both a sales number and a UN symbol. For the most part, the researcher does not need to worry about sales numbers.

For more assistance with researching UN documents, see the collection of research guides from the Dag Hammarskjöld Library.[34] These easy-to-use guides allow you to quickly figure out which resource(s) to use for your UN legal research problem.

B. LOCATING DOCUMENTS

1. Official Records

These are documents submitted to or issued by the major UN bodies during a given session or year. *The Bluebook* says you should always cite to official records, but that can be a problem since they are not published until after the session concludes. Official records include meeting records, resolutions, reports of major organs, committees, and commissions, as well as the budget and financial reports. It is easy to identify these documents since they are identified as such on the title page.

When you have a document and a document symbol, you may be tempted to conduct a Google search to locate this document on the web. While this may work some of the time, it may also lead to confusion. A better approach is to use the collections of documents provided by the UN.

2. Full-Text Documents

A quick way to locate a UN document on the web is to use https://undocs.org/ and add the UN symbol. For example, to locate UN Doc. E/CN.4/1996/52/Add.2, search: https://undocs.org/E/CN.4/1996/52/

---

34 https://research.un.org/en.

Add.2. Keep in mind that this strategy may not always work.

One of the most comprehensive collection of full-text documents is ODS (Official Document System).[35] This document system provides full-text search of documents issued since 1993; resolutions of all principal organs & Security Council plenary documents since 1946. Older documents are added regularly. Includes the Daily Journals of New York and Geneva."[36] The system does not contain press releases, UN sales publications, the United Nations Treaty Series, or information brochures issued by the Department of Public Information.

The other major tool for accessing documents is the United Nations Digital Library.[37] It contains UN documents and publications as well as information about UN materials in UN Library collections. It also provides access to many full-text documents, including resolutions adopted by the General Assembly, ECOSOC, and the Security Council from 1946 onward. The records in the database provide basic information about the UN documents and many are linked to digital files containing the complete document in official UN languages.

If you have the document symbol and it falls within the date range mentioned above, the easiest thing to

---

35 https://documents.un.org/.

36 https://research.un.org/en/docs/find.

37 https://digitallibrary.un.org/.

do is to search by symbol by typing in the document number in the box where it says "Symbol."

For example, suppose that you need the United Nations Declaration on Human Cloning, UN Doc. A/RES/59/280 (2004). Using ODS, you can simply type "A/RES/59/280" into the "symbol" box indicated above and click on "search."

By clicking on "A/RES/59/280" you can display and download the document in any of the available languages as well as obtain other information about the document, such as the complete title, publication date, and the relevant subject headings.

The main UN website[38] can also be used for obtaining some documents. Under the "Resources/Services" heading at the bottom of the homepage, select the "Documents" button, and you will be linked to the UN Documents page.[39] From this page, you can access some of the most frequently used documents: General Assembly, Security Council and ECOSOC resolutions; press releases; Secretary General reports; and other selected documents. This page also links to ODS and the UN Digital Library (mentioned above) and other collections of documents.

While ODS, the Digital Library, and the UN Documents page offer many documents, you may still need to use other tools for locating the UN document

---

38 https://www.un.org/en/.

39 https://www.un.org/en/our-work/documents.

symbol or do some searching for documents by subject or issuing body.

3. Document Indexes

The UN Digital Library[40] (mentioned above) is an electronic catalog of UN documents and publications indexed by the Dag Hammarskjöld Library and the Library of the UN Office at Geneva. It also includes commercial publications and other non-UN sources held in the collection of the Dag Hammarskjöld Library. The coverage is from 1979 onward, but older documents are added on a regular basis. This tool also allows you to find the voting records on resolutions and an index of speeches.

C. UN RESOLUTIONS

Sometimes the researcher needs primary documents, like resolutions from the major UN organs (General Assembly, Security Council, and ECOSOC). United Nations resolutions are formal expressions of the opinion or will of UN organs. They generally consist of two clearly defined sections: a preamble and an operative part. The preamble generally presents the background or motive for the resolution. The operative part states the opinion of the organ or the action to be taken.[41]

Fortunately, most of these resolutions from the General Assembly, the Security Council and the

---

[40] https://digitallibrary.un.org/.

[41] https://research.un.org/en/docs/resolutions, see the section called "UN Resolutions."

Economic and Social Council can be located from the links provided by the "About UN Documents" research guide.[42]

Resolutions are also available in the official records at the end of each session and in other print sources, like yearbooks.

D. TREATIES

Treaties are another important source of law for the legal researcher. The UN Charter mandates that every treaty and international agreement entered into by Member States must be registered with the UN Secretary General. While Member States invariably do not follow this directive, most treaties are deposited with the UN.

The official source for these treaties is the *United Nations Treaty Series* (U.N.T.S.), available in print and through the database called United Nations Treaty Collection.[43] The print version of the U.N.T.S. covers 1946–date, but the print may still suffer a small lag time. The electronic version contains all published volumes of the U.N.T.S., plus the texts of treaties in volumes not yet published, but the researcher may need to use the print version to fill in any gaps in the electronic collection.

The predecessor series is called the *League of Nations Treaty Series* (L.N.T.S.) and it covers 1920–

42 https://research.un.org/en/docs/resolutions.

43 https://treaties.un.org/.

1946; this set is available in print and through the United Nations Treaty Collection online.[44]

The United Nations Treaty Collection contains several very important additional resources, including *Status of Multilateral Treaties Deposited with the Secretary General*, the U.N.T.S. and L.N.T.S., texts of recently deposited multilateral treaties, and U.N.T.S. cumulative indexes. *Status of Multilateral Treaties Deposited with the Secretary General* contains the current status of over 560 multilateral treaties deposited with the Secretary General. This information includes the following: conclusion and entry into force dates; the participants (parties); the signature and ratification dates; the text of reservations and declarations; and a link to the text of the treaty.

Many UN treaties and agreements are available in other collections (both print and electronic); however, if possible, use the version from the U.N.T.S. since this comes from the official issuing body.

Some UN bodies provide access to specialized collections of treaties. For example, the UN High Commissioner for Human Rights (OHCHR) provides access to UN human rights treaties.[45] The UN Conference on Trade and Development (UNCTAD) provides access to bilateral investment treaties (BITs) and treaties with investment provisions

---

[44] https://treaties.un.org/Pages/Content.aspx?path=DB/LoNOnline/pageIntro_en.xml.

[45] https://www.ohchr.org/en/core-international-human-rights-instruments-and-their-monitoring-bodies.

(TIPs) through its International Investment Agreements Navigator.[46]

For more information on researching treaties, see Chapter 4 of this *Nutshell*.

8.8 OTHER LEGAL BODIES AND PUBLICATIONS

There are three bodies within the UN that focus on specific areas of international law and report to the General Assembly:

- Sixth Committee of the General Assembly, the primary forum for the consideration of legal questions;
- International Law Commission (ILC), which focuses on the progressive development and codification of international law; and
- United Nations Commission on International Trade Law (UNCITRAL), the core legal body in the field of international trade law.

Each of these bodies issues documents and reports; see the "UN International Law Documentation" research guide for an explanation of these materials.[47] Various legal publications can be searched using a "Global Search" page. This tool allows you to search several legal publications

---

[46] https://investmentpolicy.unctad.org/international-investment-agreements.

[47] https://research.un.org/en/docs/law.

simultaneously, such as yearbooks, summaries of ICJ judgments, and more.[48]

8.9 OTHER COLLECTIONS

As noted in the beginning of this section, there may be an occasion when you cannot locate a document on the web. In those instances, you may need to go to a library that has a print or microfiche collection.[49] Some libraries are designated as UN "depositories" and have more extensive collections than non-depositories. A reference librarian who works at such a depository library can be an enormously helpful guide.

Some libraries have access to the UN-iLibrary,[50] a global search and discovery tool containing publications, journals, data, and series published by UN bodies. Access the collection by theme, country, or by using the search mechanism. Some of the content is open access and freely available.

8.10 BEYOND THE DOCUMENTS: BOOKS AND ARTICLES

There will come a time when you need some commentary or analysis on topics handled by the UN or some explanation about the UN system or a particular body. Some of the better books on UN law

---

48 https://legal.un.org/globalsearch/dtSearch/Search_Forms/dtSearch.html.

49 The microfiche is published by Readex and is available in many academic libraries.

50 https://www.un-ilibrary.org/ (subscription database).

and practice are listed below. These materials are generally not freely available electronically, but they should be available in many academic law libraries.

Charter of the United Nations: A Commentary (Bruno Simma ed., 3rd ed. 2012) is the best source for commentary and analysis of the UN Charter.

Benedetto Conforti, *The Law and Practice of the United Nations* (5th rev. ed. 2016) provides legal analysis of membership, structure, origins, and practice.

Max Planck Yearbook of United Nations Law (1998–) focuses on the activities of the UN in the field of international law. Available on HeinOnline.

The Statute of the International Court of Justice: A Commentary (Andreas Zimmermann et al., eds., 3rd ed. 2019) provides an extensive commentary on the ICJ statute.

The *Oxford Handbook on the United Nations* (Thomas G. Weiss, Sam Daws, eds., 2018) provides an independent analysis by scholars of the history of the UN. Includes a chapter on law as well as specific law-related UN bodies.

Yearbook of the United Nations (1946/47–)[51] provides a detailed history of the UN for each year. It includes resolutions and gives useful references to important reports and documents. Note that this publication is many years behind. The most recent volumes are in the "Yearbook Pre-press" section of

---

[51] https://www.un.org/en/yearbook.

the website and contains draft chapters and detailed chapter research outlines for the *Yearbooks* in production.[52] Many UN bodies and institutions issue their own yearbooks, such as the *Yearbook of the International Law Commission*.[53] These yearbooks and many other UN publications are available on HeinOnline.[54]

The Audiovisual Library of International Law[55] is a unique collection of resources for research and teaching. It includes an historical archive of instruments on subjects of international law (such as criminal law, environmental law, and the law of treaties); a lecture series on various international law topics by scholars in the field; and a research library containing links to articles and resources. All of the resources are freely available.

When doing research on a topic, you may want to search library catalogs or look for articles on the topic. The United Nations Digital Library (described above) does provide information about books and articles on UN bodies and topics. Journal articles are also a good source of information on topics covered by the UN. See also the information and resources available from the Dag Hammarskjöld, like the very helpful research guides.[56] For more assistance on

---

52 https://www.un.org/en/yearbook/prepress.

53 https://legal.un.org/ilc/publications/yearbooks/.

54 United Nations Law Collection available on HeinOnline, https://heinonline.org/ (subscription database).

55 https://legal.un.org/avl/intro/welcome_avl.html.

56 https://research.un.org/en?b=g&d=a&group_id=2087.

locating relevant journal literature, see Chapter 10 of this *Nutshell*.

CHAPTER 9
OTHER INTERNATIONAL ORGANIZATIONS

9.1 INTRODUCTION

In recent decades, international organizations, meaning both intergovernmental organizations (IGOs) and nongovernmental organizations (NGOs), have developed into important players in the international legal community. Your research problem may center on one of these organizations, or you may need a document produced by one of them. Therefore, locating information that concerns them and finding their documentation is a necessary skill for one working in the area of international legal research. This *Nutshell* has already discussed the United Nations and the European Union, two international bodies which exert an enormous amount of influence in the world and issue an impressive amount of information. The focus of this chapter is to set out the basics of researching IGOs and NGOs generally and to describe some strategies for locating relevant documentation. I will provide general background and take one very large IGO, the World Trade Organization, and one very prominent NGO, Amnesty International, as exemplars.

Also note some other terms of art when researching international organizations generally: international organizations (or organisations), inter-governmental organizations, IGOs, international agencies, international institutions, non-state actors, non-governmental organizations, NGOs, and civil society.

The *Yearbook of International Organizations* includes profiles for more than 75,000 international organizations—IGOs, NGOs, and other bodies.[1] The chapter on "International Organizations or Institutions, General Aspects" in *Max Planck Encyclopedias of International Law* (2020)[2] highlights the definition from the Draft Articles on the Responsibility of International Organizations from 2011 ('DARIO'), where the International Law Commission (ILC) agreed on the following:

> The term "international organization" refers to an organization established by a treaty or other instrument governed by international law and possessing its own international legal personality. International organizations may

---

1 Available on Brill Online, https://ybio.brillonline.com/ (subscription database). Limited freely available information is available at https://uia.org/ybio/.

2 Available at https://opil.ouplaw.com/home/mpil (subscription database).

include as members, in addition to States, other entities.[3]

Most of these organizations have the following characteristics:

- An IGO has *international legal status* (privileges, immunities, rights, and duties) based upon its founding charter, constitution, or statute. As such, an IGO can enter into international agreements with other IGOs or with States.
- An IGO usually has a *legislative body*, which creates legal acts (decisions, resolutions, directives, etc.) that may bind the IGO and its Member States under international law. Most of these legislative acts do not supersede national law (except the EU).
- An IGO may have a *dispute resolution mechanism* or body which is empowered to resolve disputes among its Member States.
- The IGO usually has an *executive body* or secretariat which facilitates the operations of the IGO.

The World Trade Organization (WTO), for example, was created by the Marrakesh Treaty,

---

[3] Kirsten Schmalenbach, "International Organizations or Institutions, General Aspects" in *Max Planck Encyclopedias of International Law* (2020), https://opil.ouplaw.com/home/mpil (subscription database).

signed on April 15, 1994.[4] It has a Secretariat headed by the Director-General. The General Council is the WTO's highest-level decision-making body and meets regularly to carry out the work of the organization, whereas the topmost decision-making body is the Ministerial Conference and meets less often, at least once every two years; and the Dispute Settlement Body settles trade disputes between the Member States.[5] The members are sovereign nations, each entering the organization by choice.

An organization's founding instrument mandates many of its characteristics. These instruments can be called a treaty, convention, charter, or constitution. Most have well-developed systems for delivering documents and information.

On the other hand, organizations established by individuals or associations of individuals are called nongovernmental organizations (NGOs). NGOs are not endowed with governmental powers and cannot enter into treaties or international agreements.[6] NGOs vary in size and influence. Some of the larger groups can exercise considerable pressure in international policy debates. Often, an NGO takes an advocacy position and lobbies for its principles. NGOs

---

4 Final Act Embodying the Results of the Uruguay Round of Multilateral Trade Negotiations, Apr. 15, 1994, 1867 U.N.T.S. 14, 33 I.L.M. 1143 (1994).

5 WTO Organization Chart, https://www.wto.org/english/thewto_e/whatis_e/tif_e/org2_e.htm.

6 *Parry & Grant Encyclopaedic Dictionary of International Law* 416–17 (3rd ed. 2009). Available electronically on Oxford Reference, https://www.oxfordreference.com/ (subscription database).

such as Amnesty International and Greenpeace are good examples. Of course, not all NGOs are so high profile as these examples.

For more information on the legal intricacies of international organizations, see Alexandra R. Harrington, *International Organizations and the Law* (2nd ed. 2023) or *The Cambridge Companion to International Organizations Law* (Jan Klabbers ed., 2022).

9.2 RESEARCH GUIDES

Before starting a research problem that concerns an IGO or an NGO, it is vital that you understand the nature of the organization and the context in which it operates. Seek out a research guide or an article about the international organization that will help you understand the structure of the organization and the documentation it issues. Follow the oldest research advice in the world and know the territory before you enter it.

There is plenty of help available through research guides on the web. Simply search the name of the IGO and "research guide" using your favorite search engine. Some specific guides are available on GlobaLex, under the international law category.[7] For example, there are guides on APEC and ASEAN, the Council of Europe, ECOWAS, and the WTO. Guides on international law subjects should also be checked for sections on relevant international organizations.

---

7 https://www.nyulawglobal.org/globalex/.

Topical guides from libraries may also provide information about researching the documentation from various IGOs and NGOs. For example, Berkeley Law Library's research guide on international human rights provides in-depth information on various human rights organizations.[8]

9.3 BACKGROUND INFORMATION

When researching an international organization, you may need some "nitty-gritty" information: historical background, function, structure, addresses, names of key officials, names of member countries, and a short list of the organization's publications. If the organization has its own website, you may find what you need, but some organizations are too small, and some websites may lack relevant content. Regardless, you should know the general guides that have earned the respect of researchers. The database called Associations Unlimited database (formerly known as the *Encyclopedia of Associations: International Organizations* (1989–))[9] provides addresses, phone numbers, etc.—plus budget, membership, and publication information. See also, the Europa World database (formerly known as *The Europa Directory of International Organizations* (1999–))[10] or the *Yearbook of International*

---

8 https://libguides.law.berkeley.edu/c.php?g=326748.

9 Available electronically on Gale Directory Library, https://www.gale.com/c/associations-unlimited (subscription database).

10 Available electronically on Europa World, https://www.europaworld.com (subscription database).

Organizations (1967–),[11] both of which provide contact information as well as information about meetings, membership, and publications.

Most international organizations have some sort of web presence. A quick way of locating the appropriate website is by searching the name or acronym of the organization or by using one of the web directories mentioned above. Larger organizations use their websites as the primary mechanism for providing information about the organization and for distributing documentation.

A recent addition to the tools for researching international organizations is the Oxford International Organizations (OXIO) database.[12] The collection contains annotated documents pertaining to the law of international organizations and includes acts, key and foundational documents, treaties and more. Note that NGOs are not included in OXIO.

9.4 DOCUMENTS AND PUBLICATIONS

Many IGOs issue publications and documents of interest to the legal researcher: founding documents (treaties, charters, statutes); treaties where the IGO is a party; treaties where the IGO is the sponsor; legal acts, proceedings, and documents issued by the

---

11 Also available on Brill Online, https://ybio.brillonline.com/ (subscription database).

12 Available as part of the Oxford Public International Law collection of databases, https://opil.ouplaw.com/home/OXIO (subscription database).

IGO's legislative body; and decisions of the IGO's adjudicative body.

Again, the WTO provides a good example. By looking at its website, you locate information on the structure and functions of the organization.[13] The "WTO Documents" page provides access to its legal instruments and official documents.[14] The GATT, the predecessor of the WTO, the quasi-international organization that existed until 1995, issued documents through a microfiche collection.[15] The process for locating documents was quite cumbersome, and access to many documents was "restricted." The WTO makes many more documents available, and the best mechanism for accessing them is through the "WTO Documents Online" facility on the web.[16] Preconfigured searches can be done, usually based on the issuing body or by topic. For example, if I am interested in the accession documents for a specific country, I can click on the "By Topic" link on this website and go to "Accession to the WTO" and browse by country.[17] When I select a specific topic/country, I can run a preconfigured search, and this makes searching much more effective and efficient.

---

[13] https://www.wto.org/.

[14] https://www.wto.org/english/docs_e/docs_e.htm.

[15] Some GATT documents are available on the WTO website and through the GATT Digital Library, https://exhibits.stanford.edu/gatt.

[16] https://docs.wto.org/dol2fe/Pages/FE_Search/FE_S_S005.aspx.

[17] https://docs.wto.org/dol2fe/Pages/FE_Browse/FE_B_009.aspx.

Like the UN and EU, the WTO has an extensive document collection and uses a unique document organization system, based on symbols. There is no need to tremble when you encounter alpha-numerics such as these; see how they make sense below:

Examples of different WTO document symbols:

G/L/71

GPA/SPEC/2/Rev.1

IP/C/W/15

OFFICE(00)/39

S/ENQ/9

WT/CTE/W/31

Each symbol is made up of a combination of letters, numbers, and suffixes. Letters are used to identify collections, series, types, and the status of documents, while numbers are used to indicate sequential order. Three-letter ISO standard codes are also used to identify Members (e.g. POL for Poland, ZWE for Zimbabwe, etc.). All documents are numbered in chronological order of issue, and some documents may have more than one symbol. For more information on symbols, see "Guide to Documentation" on the WTO website.[18]

For example, IP/C/W/34/Add.3/Suppl.3—What does it all mean? That string of letters and numbers

---

[18] https://docs.wto.org/dol2fe/Pages/FE_Search/FE_S_S005.aspx.

translates as the third supplement to the third addendum to the thirty-fourth working document issued by the Council for Trade Related Aspects of Intellectual Property Rights (part of the Intellectual Property document collection):

IP = Collection

C = Series

W = Type

34; **3**; **3** = Sequential numbers

Add.; **Suppl.** = Status

The more sophisticated IGOs have intricate documentation systems like this one. Some books and research guides explain the nature and organization of these documentary systems. See *Guide to International Legal Research* (2002–) and *Information Systems of International Inter-Governmental Organizations: A Reference Guide* (1998) (good for older organizations or historical information).

Another approach to understanding these symbols would be to use a research guide, book, or an article that focuses on the organization in question. Such a guide may explain a documentation system or list depositories or libraries where research assistance is available. For example, the "WTO/GATT Research" guide[19] provides detailed guidance on both official and unofficial sources for GATT/WTO documents. Another example includes Frederic Eggermont &

---

19 https://nyulaw.libguides.com/wto_gatt.

Stafaan Smis, *Research Guide to Instruments of European Regional Organizations* (2015). But this is an area where a trained librarian may be your best bet. Do not spin your wheels—ask for help.

Be prepared to use unofficial sources that reproduce or compile important legal documents. Sometimes commentators or private publishers do a better job at making information available. Of course, when using such sources, it may be possible to access only parts of documents. Many documents issued by IGOs are in subject compilations.

Periodicals are good sources for information about documents and publications. Periodicals and reports issued by the organization are particularly informative. Articles that appear in law reviews and texts can also provide great background information; check out Chapter 10 of this *Nutshell* for help on that score.

NGOs publish many reports, newsletters, and documents that may not have a great deal of legal weight, but that are valuable to the researcher because they may document economic and social conditions and provide analysis. Such reports may focus on a particular country or on a specific topic. These materials may describe the work of the NGO or report on a particular issue or situation. Effective methods for locating such documents are using the library catalogs and secondary sources discussed elsewhere in this *Nutshell*. Many law reviews and books will cite to documents published by NGOs, especially in the area of human rights and environmental protection.

An example of an NGO with an extensive document system is Amnesty International (AI). Many libraries collect the documents and reports issued by AI, so they are publicly available in these libraries. AI has also made most of them available for free on its website.[20] Many of the documents contain a number referred to as an "Index number," for example: "Index number: ASA 39/7955/2024." This refers to the region (Asia and the Pacific) and the number of the report (the last portion indicating the year). Other index numbers may have a topical designation rather than a regional one.

When an organization's website is not easy to search or not well-organized, try using an advanced Google search.[21] The advanced search version of Google has a "site or domain" field, so you can limit your search to the organization's website URL or to something more generic, like .org or .int. For assistance locating NGOs and related information, see UC Berkeley's "Non Governmental Organizations (NGOs)" research guide.[22]

Many IGOs have digital collections of their publications, including books, papers, reports, journals, etc. While these collections used to be available only by subscription, many of these collections are now available under an open access license. These freely available collections include the

---

20 https://www.amnesty.org/en/latest/research/.

21 https://www.google.com/advanced_search.

22 https://guides.lib.berkeley.edu/NGOs.

OECD iLibrary,[23] the IMF eLibrary,[24] and the World Bank Open Knowledge Repository.[25]

9.5 LEXIS AND WESTLAW

Neither of these services provides access to much regarding IGO and NGO documentation. However, for selected IGOs, some materials are available, such as GATT and WTO panel reports.

9.6 SOME FINAL THOUGHTS

Finding documents produced by IGOs and NGOs can be difficult and frustrating. There is a general lack of good indexing, abstracting, and bibliographies for these documents. Many IGOs have their own organization and classification schemes. Even if you have what you think is a valid citation, the document may not be available on the web, but it might be available in a library's print collection. This is often the case for older documents, meaning pre-1990's. Also, sometimes the publication of official documents can be quite slow and will not appear online or in print quickly.

---

23 https://www.oecd-ilibrary.org/.

24 https://www.elibrary.imf.org/.

25 https://openknowledge.worldbank.org/home.

CHAPTER 10
COMMENTARY AND ANALYSIS

10.1 INTRODUCTION

If researching international law is new to you, consider starting your research with sources that contain commentary and analysis—books, articles, working papers, and other secondary sources. Reviewing commentary and analysis early in the research process will provide you with an introduction to an unfamiliar topic; provide citations to relevant laws and documents; allow you to gain an understanding of the terms of art and other vocabulary; and keep you abreast of new legal developments. Gaining command of the context of your research is important in any field. But on questions of international law, where intuition may lead you down the wrong path, context is of special importance.

Each day, access to e-books, electronic journals, and other web sources progresses. Still, much of the best commentary and analysis, i.e. the very contextual material that you need for international research, is primarily in print or in electronic equivalents available in subscription databases. Projects like Google Books,[1] Project Gutenberg,[2] the Internet Archives' Million Book Project,[3] and the Digital Public Library of America,[4] hold great promise. However, these projects contain few relevant sources for comprehensive international law research (not to mention for foreign or comparative law). There is more available if your library subscribes to specific e-book collections, such as The Making of Modern Law[5] or Early English Books Online.[6] These two are especially rich sets, but as such, they carry sizeable price tags and not all libraries provide access to them. Some publishers of international and comparative law books are making them available in digital libraries, like Oxford Scholarly Authorities Online[7] and Elgaronline.[8] Though it smacks of a romantic attachment to the

---

1 https://books.google.com.

2 https://www.gutenberg.org/.

3 https://archive.org/details/millionbooks.

4 https://dp.la/.

5 https://www.gale.com/primary-sources/making-of-modern-law (subscription database).

6 https://about.proquest.com/en/products-services/eebo/ (subscription database).

7 https://opil.ouplaw.com/home/OSAIL (subscription database).

8 https://www.elgaronline.com/ (subscription database).

ways things used to be, there is no substitute for a good print collection—at least not yet.

10.2 LIBRARY CATALOGS

To begin research on a topic that is unfamiliar, I recommend that most venerable of tools, the library catalog. Trust me, there are still instances where a catalog, assembled by subject specialists, will serve you better than a Google search. Be smart and search the catalogs of your own library as well as catalogs of libraries from around the country—and even around the world. The major bibliographic database in the United States is OCLC (the Online Computer Library Center).[9] OCLC includes the records of academic libraries, law firm libraries, and other libraries in the U.S. and from other countries. WorldCat,[10] is part of the OCLC's FirstSearch database of books and other materials, and it's available from many academic and public libraries in the US. One search on your computer opens the doors to collections all over the world.

Most library catalogs allow you to search by author, title, keyword, and subject. If you know of one book on your topic, you can find others by searching the subjects associated with that one source. Most catalogs also allow you to limit your search by language, date, and material type (book, journal, electronic resource, etc.). Some catalogs provide even

---

[9] https://www.oclc.org/en/home.html (subscription database).

[10] https://search.worldcat.org/.

more advanced features and value-added information, such as tables of contents, links to electronic versions of the materials, and the ability to download and save records. The librarians who assemble these online catalogs are working hard to provide you with every possible aid. In fact, many catalogs also provide QR codes[11] and links to maps that provide the precise physical location of the materials in the library stacks.

There are a few libraries outside of the U.S. that specialize in international and comparative law. It may be worthwhile to search the catalogs of these libraries to help identify relevant books and journals.

- Max Planck Institute for Comparative Public Law and International Law Catalog.[12]
- Peace Palace Library Catalogue.[13]
- Swiss Institute of Comparative Law Catalogue.[14]

While you won't be able to access the books or journals from these catalogs, they can be useful for learning about materials on your topic. Once you have located these items, check your local law library's catalog.

Books are not the only place to begin your research. Journal articles are an important part of international and comparative legal research. They

---

11 https://en.wikipedia.org/wiki/QR_code.

12 https://www.mpil.de/en/pub/library/research-tools.cfm.

13 https://www.peacepalacelibrary.nl/.

14 https://www.isdc.ch/en/library/catalogue-classification.

can provide good introductions to topics or detailed analysis. Even if you find the text of a journal article to be of little help, the article may contain citations to a plethora of both primary and secondary sources. The footnotes of a journal article are sometimes more valuable than the text; someone has done a great deal of work gathering sources for you. Of course, a journal article may also provide guidance as to the principles of customary international law.

Here is an important tip for locating a broad range of legal journal literature in international law: do not rely solely on the full-text law review collections that you find on the Lexis, Westlaw, or HeinOnline databases. If you want to do thorough research, then you must use journal indexes to locate relevant literature.

Indexes are not very popular these days. They usually require you to master a different set of search protocols and they usually give you only a citation to what you need, with no link to the text (although this is changing). This results in the dreaded two-step research process. You find the citation and then you have to go find the text.[15] But there is value in these indexes. They provide access to a broader range of journal literature and therefore include many journals that are not available full text on Lexis or Westlaw. Consequently, by searching indexes, you might locate more articles on point. With international and foreign legal research, it may be

---

[15] This is changing as journal indexes are now providing some access to the full-text articles.

the more obscure journal that contains exactly what you need.

Most journal indexes are available electronically, although each journal index operates in a slightly different manner. How to truncate words or how to use connectors ("and," "or," "within," etc.) can vary from index to index. Be sure to consult the "help" screens for information on how to search properly. (I know that no one ever actually consults the "help" screens, but I feel obliged to try to get you to do so). A few minutes spent reading this information can save you from doing countless fruitless searches.

To locate the text of the articles you find from searching the indexes, you may need to search one of the aforementioned library catalogs by the title of the journal to determine if your library subscribes to the print and/or provides access to the electronic version. It is important to note that not all journals are available electronically, and the article you want may not be available from a database. Therefore, you may need to go to a library and retrieve the print version of the journal. If your library does not have the print, check with the librarians about how to get the article you need.

10.3 LEGAL JOURNAL INDEXES

Most of the databases listed below are only available by subscription. Luckily, most law school libraries provide access to at least one of them. A few of them are also available on Lexis and Westlaw.

Index to Legal Periodicals and Books (commonly referred to as ILP). ILP contains citations from more than 1,300 legal periodicals dating from 1982 published in the U.S., Canada, Ireland, Great Britain, Australia, and New Zealand. The print edition covers 1770 to present. The web database offers two components: 1908–1981 and 1982 to present.[16] ILP is the old warhorse of legal indexes and is found in most libraries.

Legal Resource Index (commonly referred to as LRI). LRI indexes approximately 1,200 legal publications from the U.S., Canada, Great Britain, New Zealand, and Australia. Coverage begins in 1980. It is also available in print as *Current Law Index*. LRI is available on Lexis, Westlaw, and through the web as LegalTrac.[17] This database is good for searching legal newspapers and Bar Association journals.

While there is some overlap in the coverage available from ILP and LRI, it is worthwhile to search both indexes. It takes a few moments to master the search techniques each require but searching is fairly intuitive. Both tools provide some access to the full articles directly on the index platform.

Index to Foreign Legal Periodicals (commonly referred to as IFLP). IFLP is a multilingual index to

---

[16] https://www.ebsco.com/products/research-databases/index-legal-periodicals-books (subscription database).

[17] https://www.gale.com/c/onefile-legaltrac (subscription database).

articles and book reviews appearing in over 800 legal journals published worldwide. The print edition covers the period from 1960 on, and the electronic version covers 1984 to the present. IFLP is available on HeinOnline with access to many full-text articles. Since it indexes journals from all over the world, do not be surprised if you pull up an article that is not in English. IFLP has articles in 26 different languages. This index also offers a current awareness tool called IFLP Alerts.[18] Monthly Alerts notify researchers of new articles on specific topics, journals, regions, etc., but your library or institution must subscribe to IFLP for you to be able to set up Alerts.

Legal Journals Index (commonly referred to as LJI). LJI indexes over 800 journals from the UK and Europe. Coverage dates from 1986 on. The print versions of this index (*Legal Journals Index* and *European Legal Journals Index)* discontinued in 1999. *Legal Journals Index* is available on Westlaw.

When using any of the above-mentioned indexes on Lexis or Westlaw, remember that you will still need to look up the title of the journal through your library catalog or through other journal databases to access the full article.

---

[18] https://libguides.heinonline.org/index-to-foreign-legal-periodicals/iflp-alerts.

The *Current Index to Legal Periodicals* (commonly referred to as CILP)[19] is another current awareness tool providing access to over 650 primarily American legal journals. This is a good way to update your research since it indexes journals four to six weeks before they are picked up by ILP and LRI. Like IFLP Alerts, you can create a SmartCILP email notification.

10.4 LAW-RELATED JOURNAL INDEXES

At some point a legal researcher may need to search for journal articles from other disciplines, like political science, public policy, or economics. Some of the best indexes to search for articles from these areas include EconLit,[20] Worldwide Political Science Abstracts,[21] and PAIS Index.[22] There are also many full-text databases in other areas that are useful for researching legal topics. These include Contemporary Women's Issues,[23] GenderWatch,[24]

---

[19] Available on HeinOnline, https://heinonline.org/ (subscription database). See also https://libguides.heinonline.org/current-index-to-legal-periodicals.

[20] https://proquest.libguides.com/econlit (subscription database).

[21] https://proquest.libguides.com/wpsa (subscription database).

[22] https://proquest.libguides.com/pais (subscription database).

[23] https://www.gale.com/c/onefile-contemporary-womens-issues (subscription database).

[24] https://proquest.libguides.com/diversitycollection (subscription database).

and Ethnic NewsWatch.[25] For example, if you are researching property rights of women in Africa, you should search the legal literature as well as PAIS Index, Contemporary Women's Issues, and GenderWatch. Searching these databases retrieves many articles on the rights of married women in Africa from journals that would not be covered in the legal journal indexes. These databases are often available at an academic library. It's a good idea to ask a reference librarian for help in finding the right index or database and for assistance in using them.

Of course, there are some freely available web tools for locating journal literature. While none of these provides the depth of resources found in the databases listed above, they can be useful for legal research on a budget. Read on for more information.

10.5 FULL-TEXT SOURCES FOR JOURNAL ARTICLES

Lexis, Westlaw, and HeinOnline[26] all provide access to the full text of many law reviews and legal journals. None of these databases provides access to every article from every journal—and not even all US law reviews—but these three come close. Other collections are available for getting the complete text of selected articles from legal journals, including Cambridge University Press,[27] Oxford University

---

[25] https://proquest.libguides.com/diversitycollection (subscription database).

[26] https://heinonline.org/ (subscription database).

[27] https://www.cambridge.org/core (subscription database).

Press,[28] JSTOR,[29] and Elgaronline.[30] Check with your librarian for access to these and other collections of legal journal literature.

Many researchers use Google Scholar to access full-text articles. However, you won't get access to the text of subscription journals unless you are part of an institution that subscribes to the various databases. While Google Scholar is used by many researchers worldwide, you cannot limit your search results to just law journals. When using Google Scholar, use the advanced version of the search engine by clicking on "Settings" (available from the hamburger button at the top, left side of the webpage). This option allows you to search Google Scholar with more options. Researchers can set up preferences and alerts to use Google Scholar more effectively. For example, you can change the settings to display links to the full text of articles that your library or institution subscribes.[31]

Many journals are making their articles available free without any restrictions on access or use. This is called "Open Access" (commonly referred to as OA), and there are many law and law-related OA journals available. Most law schools in the U.S. and elsewhere

---

28 https://academic.oup.com/journals/ (subscription database).

29 https://www.jstor.org/ (subscription database).

30 https://www.elgaronline.com/page/82 (subscription database).

31 These instructions are for UC Berkeley, but they may be used as a guide for your own library or institution, https://guides.lib.berkeley.edu/GoogleTips/Scholar.

have created repositories for accessing the articles from law journals produced by the school, like Berkeley Law's Scholarship Repository.[32] Most of these articles can be located easily by searching Google Scholar. To locate other OA journals, see the Directory of Open Access Journals (DOAJ).[33] For a collection of many open access law journals, check out Law Review Commons.[34] Some of the indexes noted in this chapter also index open access journals. For example, IFLP indexes many OA journals, such as the *Journal of Civil Law Studies*[35] and the *Goettingen Journal of International Law*.[36] Note that some authors make their journal articles available as open access from commercial journals (those available by subscription).[37] However, not every article in an issue will be freely available.[38]

As more content is added to the web, other collections will be freely available to researchers. One such collection is called Gallica.[39] Operated by the Bibliothèque Nationale de France, Gallica is the electronic repository of nearly every periodical in France's national library. To locate the materials on

---

[32] https://www.law.berkeley.edu/library/ir/.

[33] https://doaj.org/.

[34] https://lawreviewcommons.com/.

[35] https://digitalcommons.law.lsu.edu/jcls/.

[36] https://www.gojil.eu/.

[37] An example of the open access articles policy for Brill, https://brill.com/page/articleoa/open-access-for-articles.

[38] In this example, articles that are freely available are indications by a green unlocked icon (as opposed to a red locked icon), https://brill.com/view/journals/iolr/20/3/iolr.20.issue-3.xml.

[39] https://gallica.bnf.fr/.

law, be sure to search the "droit, économie" collection. The "histoire" collection is also useful for those who are researching the history of international law. Note that most of the content is only available in French.

A small collection of academic legal journals called the International Legal Scholarship Library is available on WorldLII.[40] You can search all of the journals or select individual titles or a grouping of titles. These materials are also available on LSN (see below).

10.6 WORKING PAPERS

Another rich source for commentary and analysis is working and research papers. Scholars are making more and more of these kinds of materials available through a variety of web collections. Traditional legal publishing involves significant delays. By using one of the following series, a scholar can have his or her work in circulation quickly and can issue it as a working paper so that it need not be in final form. Some websites are becoming major repositories of such papers; others provide links to individual working paper series. The most noteworthy one is Legal Scholarship Network (LSN).[41]

Let's look at LSN more closely. LSN is part of the Social Science Research Network (SSRN), which also includes networks for accounting, economics, finance, and many more topics. Assume that you are looking for recent scholarship on "artificial intelligence" and

---

40 http://www.worldlii.org/int/journals/.

41 https://www.ssrn.com/index.cfm/en/lsn/.

"international law" (very topical at the time of updating this *Nutshell*). A simple search by title, abstract, or keywords on LSN retrieves several useful working papers and forthcoming articles on various international law issues related to AI (human rights, arbitration, autonomous weapons, and technology). It will also provide you with other useful search terms, such as large language models, machine learning, and open AI. LSN also provides access to book chapters and can be a good way to access a chapter to a book that may be unavailable through your library. A quick tip when searching LSN or any other SSRN networks, use the advanced search option.[42] It's not very advanced but it can produce better results by limiting your search terms to a specific field. Also, the full text search option is not as powerful as searching Lexis, Westlaw, or HeinOnline.

As mentioned above, many law schools have their own repositories containing the work of their faculty, including working papers or research papers. Most of these collections are search engine optimized, meaning you can locate this literature using major search engines. If you know you are interested in the work of a legal scholar at a specific institution, you can check that institution's website to see if a scholarly repository is available.

There are also many collections of working papers in other disciplines, such as National Bureau of

---

42 https://papers.ssrn.com/sol3/DisplayAbstractSearch.cfm.

Economic Research (NBER)[43] or the Grotius Centre Working Paper Series.[44] To locate more topical collections such as these, search Google or another search engine using keywords and research papers or working papers. For example, the search "international law working papers" will lead you to the Grotius Centre collection noted above.

10.7 GOOGLE SCHOLAR AND GOOGLE BOOKS

While Google Scholar and Google Books have become go-to tools for legal researchers, you need to be aware that these sources do not include everything available in print or electronic format. An example makes the point. Suppose I am interested in researching whether there is a human right to water. A search on Google Scholar retrieves some interesting results, such as an article by Leila M. Harris et al., "Revisiting the Human Right to Water from an Environmental Justice Lens," in a journal called *Politics, Groups, and Identities*. It also lists a book chapter by Inga T. Winkler called "The Human Right to Water," part of a book called *Research Handbook on International Water Law* (2019). This search also allows me to take a peek at this book using Google Books or the publisher's website. While I cannot view the entire book, I can look at the table of contents and some of the chapters to determine if

---

[43] https://www.nber.org/papers?page=1&perPage=50&sortBy=public_date.

[44] https://www.universiteitleiden.nl/en/law/institute-of-public-law/grotius-centre/research/grotius-centre-working-paper-series.

the book is on point. I can then see if a local library has the book or contemplate purchasing my own copy. To further my research, I can search the three indexes mentioned above—ILP, LRI, and LJI (on Westlaw). A search using the phrase "human rights" and water retrieves many relevant articles. Some of these citations are linked to the full text of the article on Westlaw and some are not. In fact, an interesting line of articles on this topic was published in the *Netherlands Quarterly of Human Rights*, a title which is not available in full text on Westlaw. If I had relied on just Google Scholar or full-text sources on Westlaw, I would not have discovered this body of commentary. By using both the journal indexes and the Google tools, I now know about many in-depth articles, in both legal and non-legal literature, as well as at least one relevant book. Combining research tools is always wise.

While these two Google tools, and other similar digital collections, seem to offer a lot to the researcher, you need to be aware of the limitations. Without climbing on a soapbox, here are some considerations. One example is the quality of the scanning that is at the heart of any project. It is important to note that the scanned material may not be complete or accurate. A second concern is the completeness of the material's content. Not all the content from cover to cover is freely available; you may only have access to a snippet or a section. A third issue is the ability to download, copy and paste, or print. Some sources, like Google Books, have limited output options. I advise using a library catalog to identify relevant books and then proceeding to search the various digital collections to determine if the book is available on the web, either for free or through a subscription service. Many library catalogs link to electronic versions of books and articles (either freely available or by subscription).

Even with limitations, searching Google Scholar and Google Books, along with the other tools outlined in this chapter, will make your search for commentary and analysis more fruitful. To get the most out of Google research tools, take a look at a research guide on Google search tips, such as "Google Research Made Easy."[45]

10.8 BIBLIOGRAPHIES

Using bibliographies as a research tool may seem old school; however, these lists of books and articles can be a good way to start your research. Oxford Bibliographies provides encyclopedia-like entries on various subjects within international law as well as annotated bibliographies of sources for further research.[46] The subjects range from the Arctic region to victims' rights. Other bibliographies are available in books, journal articles, and other sources on the web. For example, the International Committee of the Red Cross produces a quarterly list of references

---

[45] https://guides.lib.berkeley.edu/GoogleTips.

[46] https://www.oxfordbibliographies.com (subscription database).

to English and French publications on international humanitarian law.[47]

10.9 RANKINGS: JOURNALS AND SCHOLARS

For those interested in law journal rankings, see the Washington and Lee Law Journal Rankings website.[48] The rankings can be used by researchers to identify and compare law journals by subject, country of publication, and other categories. ScholarCheck from HeinOnline also helps you identify the most-cited journals.[49] Note that these rankings do not include all law journals across all countries.

Several tools are available to determine the ranking of a specific scholar or to identify the scholars in a particular area of law. HeinOnline, ScholarRank[50] and SSRN Top 3,000 Law Authors[51] can help with identifying top scholars in international and comparative law. Knowledge of the noteworthy scholars in your areas of interest can be useful when searching the tools noted in this chapter. You will be able to identify important scholarship

---

[47] https://www.icrc.org/en/document/international-humanitarian-law-bibliography.

[48] https://managementtools4.wlu.edu/LawJournals/.

[49] https://libguides.heinonline.org/scholarcheck/overview.

[50] https://home.heinonline.org/tools/author-profile-pages/scholarrank/.

[51] https://hq.ssrn.com/rankings/Ranking_Display.cfm?TMY_gID=2&TRN_gID=6.

through an author search as well as see what other scholars are being cited.

For an empirical analysis of international legal scholarship, past and present, see Oona A. Hathaway & John D. Bowers, "International Law Scholarship: An Empirical Study," 49 *Yale J. Int'l L.* 101 (2024).[52] Foreign and comparative law is considered one of the umbrella international law topics in Table 3 of the article.

---

52 https://yjil.yale.edu/media/51/download?inline.

CHAPTER 11

SOURCE COLLECTING AND CITE CHECKING

11.1 INTRODUCTION

Law students are often asked to collect sources and to check citations for a journal or as a professor's research assistant. These activities are very similar to normal research in international law, but the product of your research efforts will be more focused and tailored to the person who created the assignment. Though research problems are never exactly the same, I thought it would be useful to provide an overview of how to go about source collecting and cite checking. This chapter will give you some places to start and then six steps to keep in mind as you work. There is also a bit of information on where to look in *The Bluebook* for citing materials properly. All the examples in this chapter are from articles that law students had to collect and check, and they will be helpful in general international and foreign legal research as well.

11.2 SOME GENERAL SOURCES: PLACES TO START

When source collecting for a law journal article, you should be aware of the general sources that can help:

- Online catalogs set out a library's holdings and are available on most law library websites. Some folks grow sleepy at the very mention of library catalogs, but they are great resources. These library catalogs invariably include handy search tools and helpful aids. They may link you directly to the information or tell you where to find it. Many offer links to other sites that you might want to search. You should use these catalogs to locate books and journals in your own library. It is more than likely that your library gives you access to the catalogs of other libraries, too.

- Consult research guides on the web. These guides cover a variety of topics (treaties, foreign law, human rights, etc.) and are good for late-night guidance on locating sources. Remember that finding someone who has done the work for you is the aim of good researchers. If someone has already pulled together sources, use them. For example, if you are trying to research the jurisprudence of UN human rights bodies, you should check the Berkeley Law Library research guide, "International Human Rights."[1] Or, if you need to figure out how to research the law of Guatemala, try using the guide called "Legal Research in Guatemala," available on the GlobaLex website.[2]

- Many academic law libraries subscribe to databases that are useful for accessing sources and for checking citations. Databases like Foreign Law Guide, Oxford Reports on International Law, World Constitutions Illustrated, and others are enormously helpful. The bigger a library's budget, the more of these fine tools you will have access to. Ask a reference librarian if you are not sure what your library offers.

11.3 THE SIX STEPS

The following steps outline the process for locating international and foreign legal sources. Keep in mind that this is general guidance and may not work for every source. In this section, I will assume that you are source collecting and cite-checking an article for your law school journal.

---

1 https://libguides.law.berkeley.edu/c.php?g=326748.

2 https://www.nyulawglobal.org/globalex/guatemala1.html.

The six steps:

1. Review the Sources
2. Decipher the Abbreviations Used in Citations
3. Locate the International Legal Sources Contained Within the Article
4. Locate Foreign Legal Sources (Non-US Materials)
5. Locate Books and Journal Articles
6. Copy or Scan the Title Page of the Source

1. REVIEW THE SOURCES

Review all the sources you need to collect and break them down into two categories: primary sources and secondary sources. Check the text of the article when a citation is unclear. If you only have a citation or source list, ask your editors for a copy of the article—it's very helpful.

Primary sources include:

- Treaties and international agreements
- Foreign (domestic) law (statutes and case law)
- Case law from international courts and tribunals
- Documents from intergovernmental organizations (such as UN, EU, or WTO)

Secondary sources include:

- Books
- Journal articles
- Newspaper articles
- Reports
- Documents from nongovernmental organizations
- Other (working papers, conference proceedings, etc.)

For more information on primary and secondary sources in international and foreign law, see Chapter 1 of this *Nutshell*.

2. DECIPHER THE ABBREVIATIONS USED IN CITATIONS

Translate the abbreviations used in the article by using the sources listed below. If none of these tools works, ask your friendly librarian for assistance. It is best to translate them all before you start digging deeper.

- Julie Roberts Furgerson, *Prince's Dictionary of Legal Abbreviations* (10th ed. 2021).
- *The Bluebook: A Uniform Style of Citations* (21st ed. 2020). In particular, see the Tables.[3]

---

[3] https://www.legalbluebook.com/ (subscription database). Table 2 of *The Bluebook* has moved online, https://www.legalbluebook.com/bluebook/v21/tables/t2-foreign-jurisdictions. Access to this table is free even though the electronic version of *The Bluebook* is by subscription.

- Cardiff Index to Legal Abbreviations.[4] Covers many international and foreign legal sources.
- *Guide to Foreign and International Legal Citations* (2nd ed. 2009). Provides lots of information for citing and abbreviating foreign and international legal sources.
- *Noble's Revised International Guide to the Law Reports* (2002). Good for case reporters from many different jurisdictions.
- *World Dictionary of Legal Abbreviations* (1991–). Arranged by language (German, Spanish, etc.) and by subject.

There are some tools for abbreviations for specific jurisdictions, such as *Abkürzungsverzeichnis der Rechtssprache* (10th ed. 2021) for Germany.

For example, if you come across abbreviations such as BGB, ILM, or AJIL, try the Cardiff Index to Legal Abbreviations first. Each of these is easy to decipher using this freely available tool. If the Cardiff Index proves unsuccessful, try one of the other sources. If you know something about the abbreviation (a citation to a case or the jurisdiction), you might want to use one of the sources that focuses on law reports or specific jurisdictions. Of course, a web search or a search in journals on Lexis or Westlaw can often produce a fruitful result or provide more information about the abbreviation.

---

4 https://www.legalabbrevs.cardiff.ac.uk/.

3. LOCATE THE INTERNATIONAL LEGAL SOURCES CONTAINED WITHIN THE ARTICLE

Treaties and Agreements

In Step 2, you translated your citations and found that you needed a treaty. If you have a complete citation to the treaty, go directly to the cited source.

If you need a citation to a treaty or international agreement, try searching the Flare Index to Treaties[5] or consult "Frequently-Cited Treaties & Other International Instruments" research guide[6] (this site also includes a quick list of abbreviations and sources for treaties). Otherwise, consult some of the following databases to help you locate the correct citation:

- UN Treaty Collection (a database containing treaties deposited with the Secretary General and those published in the *United Nations Treaty Series*)[7]
- US Treaties and Agreements Library (HeinOnline)[8]
- United Nations Law Collection (HeinOnline)[9]
- Lexis and Westlaw

---

5 https://resources.ials.sas.ac.uk/digital/ials-digital-resources/flare-index-treaties.

6 https://libguides.law.umn.edu/frequentlycitedtreaties.

7 https://treaties.un.org/.

8 HeinOnline, U.S. Treaties and Agreements Library, https://heinonline.org (subscription database).

9 HeinOnline, United Nations Law Collection, https://heinonline.org (subscription database).

Example 1:

Your citation reads:

Agreement on Trade-Related Aspects of Intellectual Property Rights, Apr. 15, 1994, Marrakesh Agreement Establishing the World Trade Organization, Annex 1C, The Results of the Uruguay Round of Multilateral Trade Negotiations: The Legal Texts 365, *reprinted in* 33 ILM 81 (1994) [hereinafter TRIPs Agreement].

Take a look at "Frequently-Cited Treaties & Other International Instruments" research guide. From this website, the citation is provided with a link to the text of the agreement.

Agreement on Trade-Related Aspects of Intellectual Property Rights, Apr. 15, 1994, Marrakesh Agreement Establishing the World Trade Organization, Annex 1C, 1869 U.N.T.S. 299; 33 I.L.M. 1197 (1994).

Example 2:

Your citation reads:

See Vienna Convention on the Law of Treaties, 23 May 1969 [Vienna Convention], UN Doc. A/CONF. 39/27, art. 30, 1155 U.N.T.S. at 339–40.

Use the Flare Index to Treaties to confirm the citation; use the print version of the U.N.T.S. or the UN Treaty Collection to find the text of this treaty. Do note that it may be faster to get the treaty from the United Nations Law Collection on HeinOnline since you can search by U.N.T.S. citation.

See Rule 21.4 and Table 4 of *The Bluebook* for information on treaty citations and sources.

For more assistance locating the text of treaties, see Chapter 4 of this *Nutshell*.

UN Documents

If you have a UN document number (cited as "UN Doc."), try locating the document by using the following websites:

- Official Document Service (ODS).[10]

  Official UN documents from 1993; also provides access to the resolutions of the General Assembly, Security Council, Economic and Social Council, and the Trusteeship Council from 1946 onwards. Documents are available in PDF.

- United Nations Digital Library.[11]

  Search by keywords and UN document numbers. Many full-text documents are available.

Example 1:

Your citation reads:

UN General Assembly Resolution ES–10/14, *Illegal Israel actions in Occupied East*

---

[10] https://documents.un.org/prod/ods.nsf/home.xsp.

[11] https://digitallibrary.un.org/.

Jerusalem and the rest of the Occupied Palestinian Territory.

ES–10/14 means Emergency Special Session, 10th session, 14th resolution. The document, in PDF, is available from the UN Digital Library.[12]

If you have no idea what ES–10/14 means, try searching "ES–10/14 general assembly resolution" on Google. Many of the first results provide links to the text of the resolution. The UN Digital Library provides you with pretty much all resolutions.

Example 2:

Your citation reads:

United Nations Relief and Works Agency for Palestine Refugees, Report of the Commissioner-General for 1966–1967, General Assembly, Official Records, 22nd Session-Supplement No. 13 (A/6713), p. 11.

The quickest way to locate this document is to search ODS or the UN Digital Library using the document number: A/6713.[13] Search this number in the "symbol" field on the search pages of these databases. The advantage of using the Digital Library is that the URLs are stable and can be used in a citation.

---

12 https://digitallibrary.un.org/record/507734?ln=en&v=pdf.

13 https://digitallibrary.un.org/record/720304?ln=en&v=pdf.

Example 3:

Your citation reads:

S/RES/607 (1988).

Search any one of the UN websites noted above (ODS, the UN website for the main body, the UN Digital Library) to obtain a copy of the desired Security Council resolution ("RES" means resolution). Resolutions are some of the easiest documents to locate.

Example 4:

Your citation reads:

UN Doc. HCR/PC/SYR/17/01 (2017).

This looks like a UN document like the above examples. However, it was issued by the United Nations High Commissioner for Refugees (UNHCR) and the best source if the database available on its website, RefWorld.[14] A search using the document number will retrieve the needed document. You can also search the document number using Google and select the result from RefWorld.[15]

Rule 21.7 and Table 3.1 of *The Bluebook* are both useful for deciphering UN abbreviations and putting the documents into the proper citation format.

---

[14] https://www.refworld.org.

[15] https://www.refworld.org/policy/countrypos/unhcr/2017/en/118893.

For more assistance with locating UN documents, see Chapter 8.

European Union Materials

If you have citations for EU (EC or EEC are also used for earlier designations for this organization) documents, try the following sites:

- EUR-Lex[16]

  EU Law Portal that provides access to the *Official Journal* (OJ), COM documents, and almost all the legal documents you will need.

- COM documents[17]

  Commission's database; can search by number or keyword in title.

- European Court of Justice[18]

Example 1:

Your citation reads:

Markets in Financial Instruments Directive of May 15, 2014, 2014/65/EU, 2014 O.J. (L173/349).

Search the *Official Journal* (OJ) using the EUR-Lex website. This database contains the complete collection of the OJ in PDF. You can search by the OJ citation (L173/349) or by the directive number

---

16 https://eur-lex.europa.eu/homepage.html.

17 https://eur-lex.europa.eu/collection/eu-law/pre-acts.html.

18 https://curia.europa.eu/juris/recherche.jsf?language=en/#.

(2014/65/EU) using the box on the right side of the website.

Example 2:

Your citation reads:

European Parliament and of the Council on Financial Collateral Arrangements of March 27 2001, COM(2001)168 final.

Search the COM documents database noted above, available on EUR-Lex.

Rule 21.9 and Table 3.3 of *The Bluebook* are both useful for deciphering EU abbreviations and putting the documents into the proper citation format.

For more assistance with researching the EU, see Chapter 7.

WTO Documents

Use Documents Online[19] on the WTO website; no print version exists. Many GATT documents are also available from the WTO website.[20] Panel reports are commonly cited in articles (as WT/DS); here are some good sources:

- Dispute Settlement section of the WTO website.[21] Can search by document number.

---

19 https://docs.wto.org/dol2fe/Pages/FE_Search/FE_S_S005.aspx.

20 https://www.wto.org/english/docs_e/gattdocs_e.htm.

21 https://www.wto.org/english/tratop_e/dispu_e/dispu_e.htm.

- Worldtradelaw.net[22] or TradeLawGuide[23] are good sources for panel reports and other related documents and are generally easier to use than the WTO website.

Example 1:

Your citation reads:

United States—Import Prohibition of Certain Shrimp and Shrimp Products, Appellate Body Report, WT/DS58/AB/R.

This is a WTO panel report. See WTO website, worldtradelaw.net, or TradeLawGuide; locate by date, country or topic.

Rule 21.11 of *The Bluebook* covers the WTO. For more assistance with WTO documents and materials, see Chapter 9.

International Case Law

If you have a citation, decipher the abbreviation and go directly to the source by searching a library catalog for the title. Otherwise, try the website of the international court or tribunal.

To locate the website of the court or tribunal, try searching Google, WorldLII's International Courts & Tribunals Project,[24] or Worldcourts.[25] These collections cover many different international courts

---

22 https://www.worldtradelaw.net/ (subscription database).

23 https://www.tradelawguide.com/ (subscription database).

24 http://www.worldlii.org/int/cases.

25 https://worldcourts.com/.

and tribunals, but the coverage for each body varies and may not be complete.

Example 1:

Your citation reads:

Emilio Augustin Maffezini v Kingdom of Spain, ICSID Case NOARB/97/7, JAN.25 2000, 16 *ICSID Review—Foreign Investment Law Journal* 212 (2001).

Search a library catalog by the title of the journal—*ICSID Review*. Two other sources are italaw (a freely available collection of investor-state arbitration cases)[26] or the ICSID website.[27]

Note: International commercial arbitration and investor-state arbitration come up a lot when source collecting for international law journals. Consult a research guide for more guidance, such as Berkeley Law Library's research guide, "International Arbitration & Litigation."[28]

Example 2:

Your citation reads:

Legal Consequences of the Construction of a Wall in the Occupied Palestinian Territory (Advisory Opinion) [2004] ICJ Rep 136.

---

26 https://www.italaw.com/.

27 https://icsid.worldbank.org/cases/case-database.

28 https://libguides.law.berkeley.edu/c.php?g=326736.

ICJ is probably pretty familiar to you; it's the International Court of Justice. The ICJ website[29] is an easy place to get the advisory opinion (select "Advisory Proceedings") or you can consult the United Nations Law Collection on HeinOnline.[30]

Rule 21.5 of *The Bluebook* covers international law cases.

4. LOCATE FOREIGN LEGAL SOURCES (NON-U.S. MATERIALS)

Use Foreign Law Guide[31] for information about the jurisdiction and sources. The *Guide to Foreign and International Legal Citations* (2nd ed. 2009) and the *International Citator and Research Guide: The Greenbook* (2018–) can help with foreign abbreviations. See also Table 2 of *The Bluebook*[32] for help with information on selected jurisdictions.

Constitutions and Statutory Law

Example 1:

Your citation reads:

Constitution of South Africa, Chapter 2, § 39(1).

---

[29] https://www.icj-cij.org/home.

[30] HeinOnline, United Nations Law Collection, https://heinonline.org (subscription database).

[31] https://referenceworks.brill.com/display/db/flg (subscription database).

[32] Table 2 of *The Bluebook* has moved online, https://www.legalbluebook.com/bluebook/v21/tables/t2-foreign-jurisdictions. Access to this table is free even though the electronic version of *The Bluebook* is by subscription.

Most constitutions can be found in using Google or through collections, such as the Constitute Project[33] or Oxford Constitutions of the World.[34]

Example 2:

Your citation reads:

Human Rights Act, 1988, c. 42 (Eng.), in 7 Halsbury's Statutes of England and Wales 528 (4th ed. 2001).

In this case, search a library catalog for *Halsbury's Statutes of England and Wales*. If no source is cited, consult Foreign Law Guide or a research guide for ideas on where statutes are published for specific jurisdictions. In this case, you can use the British and Irish Legal Information Institute (BAILII)[35] or Legislation.gov.uk.[36]

National Case Law

Example 1:

Your citation reads:

Ireland K(C) v K(J), [2004] 1 ILR 224.

Decipher the abbreviation and get the title of the reporter. Search a library catalog by the name of the publication—*International Law Reports*. ILR is also available on the vLex database.[37]

---

33 https://www.constituteproject.org/.

34 https://oxcon.ouplaw.com/ (subscription database).

35 https://www.bailii.org/.

36 https://www.legislation.gov.uk/.

37 https://vlex.com/ (subscription database).

Example 2:

Your citation reads:

In re Ning Yi-Ching, 56 T. L. R. 3 (Vacation Ct. 1939).

Decipher the abbreviation and look up the title of reporter. Search a library catalog by the name of the publication—*Times Law Reports*. This case is also reprinted in *the Annual Digest and Report of Public International Law Cases* (1942).[38]

Example 3:

Your citation reads:

Decision of French Cour de Cassation, *reprinted in* XXIV I.L.O.M. 360 (1984).

There is no such source as I.L.O.M.; the citation should be 24 I.L.M. 360 (1985). Do not spend hours trying to figure out abbreviations—ask a librarian.

Some national case law may be available on the web or in journal literature. Keep in mind that case law can be difficult to obtain and may not be available in English. For further assistance with researching non-US law, see Chapter 3.

The Bluebook does not provide guidance for many non-US legal jurisdictions. When a country is not covered in Table 2, see Rule 20. This rule covers the

---

[38] Available from Cambridge Law Reports Collection (subscription database).

basics: constitutions, statutes, cases, etc. Use the examples as templates.

5. LOCATE BOOKS AND JOURNAL ARTICLES

Search for books and journals by using library catalogs or WorldCat (a database of libraries around the globe, good for determining if a title exists and which library owns it).[39] Search by author or title first, and then try keyword searching. In most catalogs, keyword searches include author names, editor names, and words from the title. Sometimes citations in articles are incorrect, so always check the title by doing a keyword search. Be sure to drop the initial article when searching by title. See Rule 15 and of *The Bluebook* for information on books and articles.

Book Chapters

Example 1:

Your citation reads:

Don Greig, "International Community", "Interdependence" and All That . . . Rhetorical Correctness?, in *State, Sovereignty, and International Governance* 521, 530–31, 566 (Gerard Kreijin et al., eds., 2002).

Look up the title of the book on a library catalog (*State, Sovereignty, and International Governance*). The clue here is the word *in*—usually, you cannot

---

[39] https://search.worldcat.org/.

look up the chapter; you must look up the title of the book.

Books

Example 1:

Your citation reads:

PH Fouchard et al., *Traité de l'Arbitrage Commercial International* (1996).

Look up the author or the title on a library catalog.

Example 2:

Your citation reads:

Nye, Joseph S., *Bound to Lead: The Changing Nature of American Power,* New York: Basic Books, 1990.

You can search a library catalog by author or title.

Tip: as more books become available on the web, you may have luck locating the book or the chapter through online collections, such as Google Books. Some libraries subscribe to electronic book collections too.

Legal Journals

Sometimes citation information will be incomplete, incorrect or you will need to decipher an abbreviation. Use one of the journal indexes to get accurate information; see Chapter 10 for more information:

- Index to Legal Periodicals and Books (ILP)[40]
- Legal Resource Index (LRI)[41]
- Index to Foreign Legal Periodicals (IFLP)[42]
- Legal Journals Index (LJI)[43]

Example 1:

Your citation reads:

Benedict Kingsbury, "The Tuna-Dolphin Controversy, the World Trade Organization and the Liberal Project to Reconceptualize International Law," 5 *Y.B. Envt'l L.* 1, 10 (1994).

Search a library catalog for the title of the publication—*Yearbook of International Environmental Law*.

Example 2:

Your citation reads:

Pierre Legrand, "Civil Law Codification in Quebec: A Case of Decivilianization," 1

---

[40] https://www.ebsco.com/products/research-databases/index-legal-periodicals-books (subscription database).

[41] Available on Lexis, Westlaw, and on the web as LegalTrac, https://www.gale.com/c/onefile-legaltrac (subscription database).

[42] Available on HeinOnline, https://heinonline.org/ (subscription database).

[43] Available on Westlaw.

Zeitschrift für Europäisches Privatrecht 575 (1993).

Search a library catalog for the title of this German periodical—*Zeitschrift für Europäisches Privatrecht*.

6. COPY OR SCAN THE TITLE PAGE OF THE SOURCE

It's good practice to copy (scan or download) the title page or jot down the name and date of the source on the copy. This will help you out a lot at 3:00 am. Don't assume that if you found it once on the web, you can find it again. If you find it, download it and save it!

11.4 ELECTRONIC SOURCES

Electronic sources are acceptable if no print source is available. Be sure to use the best (most authoritative) electronic version possible. Check with your journal editors for the policy on electronic versions of print materials.

11.5 SOME CITE-CHECKING TIPS

Since *The Bluebook* is not always adequate for citing international and foreign legal materials, use the examples in *The Bluebook* as models. Be sure to include enough information so that someone else can find the cited materials. Also, be consistent throughout the entire document.

- For help with proper abbreviations and formats, see the tables at the back of *The Bluebook*.

- When you cannot find any guidance in *The Bluebook*, look at other examples from other top law reviews.

- If you cannot locate a source using catalogs and other databases, try searching full-text journals on Lexis or Westlaw to see if someone else has cited the same source. There may be a better citation or a clue that will help you locate the materials.

- When citing to an electronic version of a document, be sure to follow rule 18 of *The Bluebook*.

Finally, when stymied or confused, ask for help. As stated throughout this *Nutshell*, that's why librarians are there.

CHAPTER 12
GENERAL RESEARCH STRATEGIES

12.1 INTRODUCTION

If the subject of this *Nutshell* is international and foreign legal research, why would there be a chapter about general research strategy? Think of your author as a missionary who preaches a gospel of good research habits. I hope that you have developed solid researching skills from your general experience with legal materials, but at the very least, I want to reinforce them. As you gain experience as a legal researcher, your skills, habits, and methodology will also develop. Working with international and foreign legal materials can help you reflect on your more general research habits and patterns. And there is the view that like green, leafy vegetables and regular exercise, good research skills are just good for you.

An important first step is to recognize that "research" describes a pretty wide range of activity. Sometimes research is a simple act of finding a specific document, like locating a definition or verifying a date. It could be that you want to find a particular treaty or agreement. Other times, research can involve a complex process in which you consult numerous sources and synthesize and analyze what you find. Before doing anything else, decide what it is that you want to do.

Listed below are seven general research strategies (and habits) you should follow, no matter what your research project might be. Research is not a linear process, and you will not follow each stage and move on to the next. You will constantly be going back and forth between stages during the research process, and, for some of us, that makes it fun. It is also why note taking is crucial. Over time, you will develop strategies that work best for you, and those strategies will vary depending on the project, the time allowed for the project, and the resources that are available. At that point, you will be an expert. Be sure to help those who come asking for assistance.

12.2 THE STEPS

1. THINK BEFORE YOU BEGIN YOUR RESEARCH

A little preparation and thought before you jump into a research project can save time and be very valuable—really. Take a few moments to think about your research project. Most human beings want to plunge right into a project; they do not want to think about what they are going to do. They want to just do it. (This must be related to everyone's hatred for reading the directions before using their new cell phones). But be a good economist. A little time invested at the beginning of your research can save a great deal of time later in the process. Overcome that desire to dive in without a plan, and it will pay off. This will be a very good habit to develop when you begin to use AI for research.

Consider the following points:

- What are you trying to accomplish or what do you need to research? Try to imagine your ideal answer. What do you want?

- What information do you have before you start? Do you know the relevant law or the relevant facts? Since your research problem was quite likely generated elsewhere, i.e. handed to you by a professor or a senior lawyer in your organization, get as much information from them as possible. It is amazing how often folks miss the opportunity to explore the parameters of the research query with the person posing it. Be a good interviewer.

- What do you think you need to locate? Is there relevant primary law that you need to locate, such as a treaty or international agreement, national legislation, or case law? Do you need to locate facts such as dates or names? This will determine your direction—it is crucial.

- How much time do you have to spend on this project? This may be dictated by a self-imposed deadline, a paper due date, how much billable time can be spent on the project, or a deadline imposed by a supervisor. Frequently, resources will dictate how much time you can spend and what kind of sources you can use. If you have access to expensive databases, you will be doing one kind of research; if you can only use resources freely available on the web, it will be quite different.

- Locate print and electronic research guides and bibliographies. My research mantra is: find someone who has done the work for you! There are many altruistic souls who have compiled guides, and there are many scholars who have exhaustively gathered sources. If someone has done this in your area of interest, find it. Research guides highlight resources and may provide some information regarding research strategy. Traditional bibliographies simply highlight relevant resources.

- Keep good notes of what you have done during your research process. I do not mean to offend you by repeating advice that may have been provided to you by an elementary school teacher, but good notes are crucial. I shudder at the thought of the legion of folks who have had to retrace their own paths because they forgot where they had gone. It sounds banal, but keeping good notes can be efficient and save you time in the end.

- Write down the keywords or terms of art that may be useful. If someone gave you this question to work on, they might be a good source. Secondary sources with good indexes can help. Asking a librarian can also work. If you do not know the keywords or the names of important concepts, you can spin your wheels for a long time.

- Make a list of the resources you think you want to consult (specific databases and print resources). Be sure to note the ones you have used and what terms you searched. If something was particularly useful, note that as well. It is also useful to note idiosyncrasies in the tools you use, for future reference. This is how you become an expert.

- Prepare a list of the sources as you consult them (like a bibliography). Include the basic bibliographic information (often referred to as metadata) (title, publisher, publication date, any information on updates). When including information about an electronic source, include the searches used, the dates searched, and any other relevant information. The date you last viewed the source can be incredibly important.

See Chapter 14 of this *Nutshell* on effectively using technology for legal research. These tools can help you collect and organize your research.

Don't get sidetracked.

- It is easy to locate something else of interest and veer off in another direction. Stay on point. Unless it is a really good cat video.

2. SECONDARY SOURCES ARE YOUR FRIENDS

Many researchers think that locating the relevant primary source is the most important first step. American law school pedagogy is built around this idea, so it is not surprising. However, many times you don't know what sources of law are needed or you do not understand the scope of the issues involved. Background or secondary sources can be the best place to start when researching a new issue or unfamiliar area of law because these sources discuss and analyze the law. Sometimes, these sources will even reprint the portions of the primary source that you are after. Secondary sources include books, encyclopedias, journal articles, etc. They are online and in print. Even if a source is not something that you would cite to in a brief or include in an article, it may still be useful in explaining background, defining terms, and providing citations to other materials.

Locate and review secondary sources.

- Search for law books and articles on your topic using library catalogs, indexes, and other databases. Here I am counting on you to have some basic research skills. Individual chapters in this *Nutshell* discuss relevant databases, websites, indexes, and catalogs. I have given you as much specific guidance as possible, but you must be willing to make full use of the tools discussed.

- Review what you have gathered and take notes. Print out or download important pages that you find online. Photocopy or scan the title page and noteworthy pages of paper sources or make note of the bibliographic information and the relevant pages. To repeat our refrain, doing this when you first encounter the information will save you time later.
- Note any citations to international and foreign laws, including case law.
- Note references to other articles, books, and similar materials. Consult these sources as well. Also make a list of the scholars who have written these books and articles.

3. PRIMARY SOURCES OF LAW—THE HEART OF THE MATTER

Primary sources are the law—statutes, case law, regulations, treaties, etc. When researching foreign and international law, keep in mind that each legal system is a snowflake in that no two are exactly the same. I guide you to sources that will help you find out the sources in each system. Be sure to use them.

Locate the primary sources of law.

- Locate the law cited to in the secondary sources. These sources include treaties, national laws and regulations, and case law.
- Locate an annotated source for legislation (an annotated code or commentary), if possible. This may lead you to relevant case law.
- Once you locate one case on point, remember that it is a research document itself. It discusses how the relevant judicial body viewed a particular issue at a given moment in time. It should contain citations to all relevant documents. It should lead you to other cases, treaties, etc.
- If you need an English-language translation, try to locate that as well.
- Once you have some law to start with, look for other related primary sources.

4. REMEMBER THAT NON-LEGAL SOURCES MAY BE CRUCIAL

- You may need non-legal information, such as dates, statistics, and economic or political data. Once again, the indexes and secondary source material discussed in the various chapters of this *Nutshell* will help you out. A good journal article in a non-legal publication might provide invaluable background information. International law exists in the world of international politics and relations.

Consult newspapers and other non-legal sources to get context, especially for recent events.

5. MAKE SURE YOUR RESEARCH IS UP-TO-DATE

- Is the source that you are citing current? If you are using a database, when was it updated? When was the website modified?
- If using books, be sure to consult pocket parts or supplements, if available. American legal researchers are accustomed to fast and almost seamless updating of materials. International and foreign legal materials may move more slowly and be updated at a slower pace. Know the vintage of what you are using.
- Keep in mind that there are not always electronic databases to check for updates to laws of other jurisdictions. Indeed, most jurisdictions do not have equivalents to Shepard's (Lexis), Keycite (Westlaw), or BCite (Bloomberg Law). American legal information is by far the most developed; do not assume that other countries or international bodies have similar research tools. The internet allows the researcher to do some incredible research, but the variation in available research tools is stunning.

6. THE BIG QUESTION—HOW DO I KNOW WHEN I AM DONE?

- There is no easy answer to this question. It just depends. Go back to the issues outlined when you thought about the project. Have you used all your time? Is the deadline approaching, and it is time to write the paper or file the brief? This is why you need a plan. Do you want to hear sad stories about researchers who waited too long or who did not know when to stop and ended up with nothing when the deadline came upon them? I didn't think so. Never forget your allotted time and resources. These usually dictate whether you are done.
- If you start seeing the same sources over and over and you feel you have done a thorough job on the research, you may be done. Many questions do not have answers. If you see the same dilemma over and over, you have probably reached the end. This is the good part; you get to produce your view on the matter.

7. ASK FOR HELP

Ask a reference librarian at your school, institution, law firm, or organization, or call someone in an academic law library. Reference librarians live to serve. They want to help you. What may seem the like the world's most complex problem to you might be something that a good reference librarian can solve in seconds (okay, minutes). Use them. At the very least, it is helpful to review your project with an information professional to make sure you have covered the basics. Remember, librarians are always on your side.

12.3 RESEARCH PLAN

As noted above, it's always a good idea to take a few minutes before you begin your research and create a research plan. A plan is even more important for tight time deadlines, although it may not seem like you have the time. A few minutes spent on a research plan can save you time and keep you on track.

Your research plan should identify the question(s) you are trying to answer and sets out a strategy of where to look (see the steps noted above). Have note taking and organizational tools ready.

A research plan can take many forms. It could be scribbled notes on a piece of paper or sticky note, or a more formal approach using Word or Excel. A research plan can also be the basis of a research log. A research log is a record of your research process, and it can be used to take notes about how and where you found useful materials and how you plan to use them in your research. A log is also a good place to note useful sources to go back to later as you refine your project with additional research and analysis. And here's a bonus, creating a log can also help you build your overall research expertise. Here is a useful list for your log:[1]

1. **Keywords** from thinking, brainstorming, background reading, or a thesaurus. [Consider synonyms and alterative terms of art.]

2. **Relevant call numbers**, to use for both shelf and online browsing purposes.

3. **Subject headings** from the full display in an online catalog *and* subject descriptions from every relevant article database. [Many online sources now provide descriptive tags and metadata that can be used as search terms.]

4. **Authors and scholars** whose work is repeatedly mentioned by others.

5. **Titles of peer-reviewed journals** and popular journals.

6. **Titles of relevant reference tools** related to the research project.

7. **Publishers** that seem to specialize in the field.

8. **Institutions, associations, societies, or government agencies** that focus on the area of interest.

---

1 Mary W. George, "A More Complete List of Lists Every Researcher Should Keep," in *The Elements of Library Research* 82 (2008).

9. **Dates**, such as the life span of key people, the exact date of a major event, or the publication year of primary sources.
10. **Order of the steps** taken to obtain background information and discover sources, including the navigation path leading to electronic resources and the address of useful web pages.

A research log should also contain the following elements:

- Dates when you did your searching. This is very useful if you need to come back to a project later.
- Where you searched (search tools and sources). This helps you avoid redoing your research.
- Search strategies that were useful (and even those searches that were not productive, so you don't repeat those same fruitless searches).
- Ideas to pursue during the next research session.
- Any other notes that will help you be more productive and efficient.

For some tips on tools that may be useful for creating a research log or taking notes on a research plan, see Chapter 14.

AI is seeping into the legal research realm and cannot be ignored. I cover a bit of AI research basics in Chapter 14. However, using AI for research does not negate all the advice regarding research strategies and planning noted above and throughout this *Nutshell*.

CHAPTER 13
STAYING AHEAD OF THE CURVE

13.1 INTRODUCTION

Now that you have made it to the end of this *Nutshell*, one crucial question remains: how do you stay on top of new resources? You know that even as you read this sentence, someone is creating a new website or writing a new article that is relevant to your topic. And how can you possibly keep track of new legal developments? Not to worry; I will clue you in on a few tools and a bit of technology that will allow you to monitor websites, follow organizations and individuals, and stay up-to-date. Please note that these entries are a small sampling of the available websites, newsletters, blogs, social media feeds, etc. I encourage you to explore further and develop your own list of resources to monitor.

13.2 NEW DEVELOPMENTS

These tools are good for keeping track of new developments and topics within international and comparative law. Every field develops a set of publications that are read by everyone who works in the area. Most of these sources do not have the depth of a journal article, but they benefit from being frequently updated and current. If everyone who matters is reading them, then you will be a part of the cutting edge. Skimming these can make you look smart.

ASIL Insights
https://www.asil.org/insights
Brief outlines and analyses of new developments or significant events in international law. You can subscribe via email or RSS feed. This is a fine way to keep yourself on top of new developments.

Global Legal Monitor
https://www.loc.gov/collections/global-legal-monitor/about-this-collection/
An electronic publication of the Law Library of Congress that is intended for those who have an interest in legal developments from around the world. The Law Library of Congress is a tremendous resource. It employs legal specialists from all over the globe, and it is responsible to Congress. You pay the salaries of the specialists, so use them.

International Enforcement Law Reporter (1985–)
http://www.ielr.com/
A monthly newsletter that tracks and summarizes key developments in international law and related areas. Topic areas generally include money laundering, drug trafficking, taxation, extradition, asset forfeiture, human rights, cybercrime, and intellectual property. For access to complete content, you must subscribe.

International Law in Brief
https://www.asil.org/ilib
A blog providing updates on new developments in international law, such as new treaties or cases.

Lexology
https://www.lexology.com
A terrific source of international and comparative legal updates. Some articles provide in-depth analysis of an issue. While not academic in nature, the articles are usually written by practicing lawyers and other legal professionals. Available in multiple languages.

Mondaq
https://www.mondaq.com/
Another good way to learn about new legislation and other legal updates around the world. Comparative guides are also available.

13.3 BLOGS

Blogs continue to be important sources for learning about current legal developments and staying up on new information. Blogs may provide even more up-to-date coverage than the sources mentioned above. Some blogs provide analysis and commentary, and others report on new issues and ideas. Here are some useful international and foreign law blogs:

Conflict of Laws.net
https://conflictoflaws.net/
This blog covers conflict of laws (or private international law) around the globe. It covers research, cases, publications and more.

DipLawMatic Dialogues
https://fcilsis.wordpress.com/
The blog of the Foreign, Comparative & International Law Special Interest Section of the American Association of Law Libraries (AALL).

EJIL: Talk
https://www.ejiltalk.org/
Blog of the European Journal of International Law.

European Law Blog: News and Comments on EU Law
https://europeanlawblog.eu/
This blog aims to highlight, and comment on, current developments in EU case law and legislation.

In Custodia Legis (Law Library of Congress)
https://blogs.loc.gov/law/
The posts on this blog often deal with foreign and international legal issues. For an example, see "Bite-Sized Legal Research Tutorial: Foreign Legal Gazettes Guide."[1]

International Law Reporter
https://ilreports.blogspot.com/
A good resource for learning about new articles, papers, books, etc.

IntLawGrrls
https://ilg2.org
"IntLawGrrls aims to give voice to women scholars, lawyers, policymakers, leaders, activists, on issues related to international law, policy and practice, from arbitration to human rights to trade, among other topics of expertise." The felicitous title cues you in that you may find some provocative thinking on this one.

Lawyering Justice Blog: Report from the Hague
https://www.publicinternationallawandpolicy group.org/blog
Reports on matters of international criminal justice, human rights, and technology for redress. Includes news updates and analysis of international law issues.

---

[1] https://blogs.loc.gov/law/2024/07/bite-sized-legal-research-tutorial-foreign-legal-gazettes-guide/.

Opinio Juris
https://opiniojuris.org/
This blog is one of the first dedicated to international legal issues and the authors include academics, practitioners, and other international legal experts. Also produces podcasts.

Of course, as with everything else, there are topic-specific blogs, too, such as:

Forced Migration Current Awareness Blog
https://fm-cab.blogspot.com/

International Economic Law and Policy Blog
https://worldtradelaw.typepad.com/

Just Security
https://www.justsecurity.org/

Kluwer Arbitration Blog
https://arbitrationblog.kluwerarbitration.com/

LawFare
https://www.lawfaremedia.org/

Legal History
https://legalhistoryblog.blogspot.com/

Legal Technology Blogs

3 Geeks and a Law Blog
https://www.geeklawblog.com/

The Brainyacts
https://thebrainyacts.beehiiv.com/

Dewey B Strategic
https://www.deweybstrategic.com/

LawSites
https://www.lawnext.com/

Because there are so many blogs to keep up with, consider subscribing to updates through email, RSS feeds, or follow them on social media.

To locate more blogs, you can do some web searches using your favorite search engine or consult a directory of blogs.[2]

13.4 NEWSLETTERS

Yes, these still exist. Bloomberg Law[3] offers a host of newsletters and email updates on several international law topics: environment, intellectual property, trade, securities, and the WTO. Another example is Competition Policy International (CPI), a subscription newsletter (and journal) containing news and information on competition and antitrust worldwide.[4] Academic law libraries and law firms subscribe to many of these sources.

13.5 PEOPLE

People are still great resources. Try Jumpstart Your Foreign, Comparative, and International Research.[5] Another way to reach people around the

---

2 Justia BlawgSearch, https://blawgsearch.justia.com/.

3 https://news.bloomberglaw.com/ (subscription database).

4 https://www.pymnts.com/cpi (subscription database).

5 https://www.aallnet.org/fcilsis/resources-publications/research-resources/jumpstart/.

world is through the INT-Law listserv.[6] Questions vary from specific research questions to locating a copy of an article from a journal from another jurisdiction. People from around the world monitor this list, and they are always helpful and informative.

Videos are another way to learn from people, and many are available on YouTube. Yes, you can watch something educational in between cat videos. Simply search for your topic, and you will find all kinds of videos. You may want to search for a specific international law expert or a law school to help you locate some of the better videos. Don't know who the experts are? Try the UN's Audiovisual Library of International Law.[7] This site contains a series of lectures on many topics given by international law scholars from around the world. All for free!

Even if you don't have a local expert to ask, such as a knowledgeable librarian, you can email the experts, such as the librarians at the UN:

> United Nations, Ask DAG
> https://ask.un.org/
> Questions and answers about the United Nations and the library resources.

13.6 PODCASTS

If you cannot ask a question directly of an expert, a podcast may be the next best thing. Podcasts are

---

[6] http://www.slaw.ca/2018/03/13/the-int-law-email-discussion-list-migrates-to-google-groups/.

[7] https://legal.un.org/avl/intro/welcome_avl.html.

usually free, timely, and can provide quite a bit of interesting insight. Here are just a few:

ASIL, International Law Behind the Headlines
https://www.asil.org/podcast
Top international law experts discuss current issues in the news.

EJIL:LIVE!
http://ejil.org/live.php
The editors of the European Journal of International Law offer another forum for analysis on international and national legal issues.

Jus Cogens: The International Law Podcast
https://podcasters.spotify.com/pod/show/jus-cogens-podcast
"A casual stroll into the unwieldy world of International Law, struggling to keep up with whims of global politics and international relations."

13.7 FOLLOWING THE EXPERTS

There is so much current information on various web outlets on international law, comparative law, and related topics—I barely scratched the surface. Anyone wishing to stay on top of new information needs to be an avid reader of global news and follow the flow of new legal scholarship. Many international law experts can be followed on X[8] and other social media platforms. By using social media, you can

[8] https://x.com/. To learn about alternatives to X, see https://brand24.com/blog/twitter-alternatives/.

explore different topics of interest, like #Internationallaw, or you can follow people and organizations, such as the @UnitedNations.

Keep track of new scholarship by signing up for an RSS feed on Legal Scholarship Network[9] or by creating an Author Alert on HeinOnline.[10] If your library subscribes to Current Index to Legal Periodicals (CILP) or Index to Foreign Legal Periodicals, you can get a list of new journal articles delivered to your email.[11] See Chapter 10 for more details on these services.

No matter your preference for learning about new information and current scholarship, don't forget the amazing librarians all over the world who are (usually) happy to point you in the right direction. A box of chocolates helps, too.

---

9 https://www.ssrn.com/index.cfm/en/lsn/.

10 https://help.heinonline.org/kb/author-profile-pages/.

11 https://libguides.heinonline.org/current-index-to-legal-periodicals/smartcilp and https://libguides.heinonline.org/index-to-foreign-legal-periodicals/iflp-alerts.

CHAPTER 14

TECHNOLOGY AND LEGAL RESEARCH

14.1 INTRODUCTION

In recent years, many tools have emerged to assist the legal researcher in a variety of ways: more effective web searching; managing and organizing information and sources; citing to web sources efficiently; and making research faster and more effective by using artificial intelligence (AI). In this section, I outline some of the tools available for each of these research activities.

14.2 SEARCH ENGINES

Most researchers use Google for searching the web.[1] While this is often very effective, it is useful to consider other search engines. One of the reasons is the claim by developers and researchers that Google

[1] Review this research guide on ways to search Google more effectively, UC Berkeley Library, "Google Research Made Easy: Advanced Searching in Google," https://guides.lib.berkeley.edu/GoogleTips.

has been more selective when it indexes the web (this indexing is what allows you to locate information and websites). For more information on this issue, see "Google's Increasing Selectivity: Effects on Information Access and Diversity."[2] As this blogpost states, using other search engines can help mitigate some of the impact of the changes with Google. Consider using DuckDuckGo (especially good on privacy issues), Bing, or another search engine (there are a bunch).[3] If you really want to dig into the "deep web" (not to be confused with the dark web) and locate other sites for research, see the annual "Deep Web Research and Discovery Resources," by Marcus P. Zillman.[4]

While artificial intelligence (AI) tools are covered in section 14.5 below, I do want to note that AI-powered search engines are beginning to challenge traditional search engines. One such search engine that has been praised by reviewers is called Perplexity[5] and there are several others.[6] Google

---

[2] Criminal Law Library Blog, August 4, 2024, https://www.criminallawlibraryblog.com/googles-increasing-selectivity-effects-on-information-access-and-diversity/.

[3] Search Engine Journal, February 12, 2024, "23 Great Search Engines You Can Use Instead of Google," https://www.searchenginejournal.com/alternative-search-engines/271409/#close.

[4] "Deep Web Research and Discovery Resources," compiled by Marcus Zillman, https://deepweb.us/. See also, Zillman's annual "Guide to Searching the Internet," https://www.searchingthe internet.info/.

[5] https://www.perplexity.ai/.

[6] Sabrina Ortiz, "The Best AI Search Engines of 2024: Google, Perplexity, and More," May 7, 2024, https://www.zdnet.com/article/best-ai-search-engine/.

also provides "AI overviews" when you use the search engine (although it's still considered experimental).

14.3 ORGANIZING AND MANAGING YOUR RESEARCH

As noted in Chapter 12, using a research log is an efficient habit to develop and some of these tools may help you organize the information you locate when searching catalogs, databases, and websites. Many of these resources are freely available and easy to download and use.

Note-taking tools

- Evernote
  https://evernote.com/
- Notion
  https://www.notion.so/notes
- Obsidian
  https://obsidian.md/
- OneNote (Microsoft)
  https://www.onenote.com/ (There is a freely available version.)
- Word, Excel, Google Docs, Google Sheets
- Research notebook, index cards (You know, some sort of paper and a pen—old school but still effective.)

Citation management tools

The following programs help collect, manage, organize, and create citations. For a comparison of some of these tools, see "Manage Your Citations," a research guide from the UC Berkeley Library.[7]

- EndNote (subscription) https://endnote.com/
- Mendeley https://www.mendeley.com/
- Power Notes (subscription)[8] https://www.powernotes.com/
- Reworks (subscription) https://proquest.libguides.com/refworks
- Zotero https://www.zotero.org/

Zotero is a very powerful, open-source citation management tool, so you may want to read more about it to take full advantage of its features.

- Zotero Research Guide (UC Berkeley Library) https://guides.lib.berkeley.edu/zotero
- Zotero for Law Students and Scholars (Washington and Lee Law Library) https://libguides.wlu.edu/c.php?g=99586&p=644177

[7] http://guides.lib.berkeley.edu/publichealth/citations. Compares Endnote, Zotero, and Mendeley. While Refworks is not covered in this research guide, it is available through some libraries.

[8] PowerNotes is a research organization and outlining tool that uses a browser extension to capture, organize, and track sources from library catalogs, databases, and websites.

- Juris-M (A Zotero-variant that has been modified to support legal writing and multilingual research.) https://juris-m.github.io

For more assistance with Zotero and Juris-M, search for and check out the many research guides available on the web.

Storing files and documents

These tools are all free (at least the basic versions) and provide secure storage available from anywhere and are good for collaborative projects. Check with your library to determine if your institution offers free storage on any of these systems.

- Box
  https://www.box.com/home

- Dropbox
  https://www.dropbox.com/

- Google Drive
  https://www.google.com/drive/

A final note, most of the tools and applications mentioned in this chapter require setting up an account. Do yourself a favor and start using a password manager, like LastPass or 1Password. The basic versions of these applications are often free. Check out some of the "best password managers" articles on the web.[9] Your school or institution may offer a password manager for free.

14.4 STABLE URLs AND DOIs

Bad and dead links are the bane of the modern researcher. Fortunately, there are some ways to help mitigate this frustration. Many websites and databases now provide stable URLs (also called permalinks, permanent links, or persistent links). These links are considered reliable and unique. Some tools for stable URLs include Digital Object Identifiers (DOI)[10] and Permalinks.[11]

For example, JSTOR provides a "stable URL" on the front page of every article. The EU law database, EUR-Lex, provides a permanent link for each document.

You will find these stable URLs in books and articles, and you can use them when citing sources for papers, law journals articles, legal memos, etc. These stable URLs are often shorter and don't look so messy when cited in a book or article.

---

9 For example, see https://www.pcmag.com/picks/the-best-password-managers?test_uuid=001OQhoHLBxsrrrMgWU3gQF&test_variant=a; https://www.nytimes.com/wirecutter/reviews/best-password-managers/; or https://www.cnet.com/tech/services-and-software/best-password-manager/.

10 https://www.doi.org/.

11 https://perma.cc/.

14.5 ARTIFICIAL INTELLIGENCE AND LEGAL RESEARCH

Artificial Intelligence (AI) is much on the minds of legal researchers. Of particular interest is generative AI (GenAI), which refers to AI systems that create new content based on prompts and inputs.[12] This edition of the *Nutshell* is being revised during the summer of 2024. By the time you read this, it will probably be early 2025. Anything I write here may be dated so I will attempt to provide some information on AI tools that will assist with international and foreign legal research, give some broad research advice, and provide suggestions for further reading. I will not cover general purpose AI tools, like ChatGPT, since there are many other places to get this information. In the space where legal research and technology meet, you will want to discuss AI tools and issues with a law librarian.[13]

Currently, the big players in legal research, Lexis, Westlaw, and Bloomberg Law (and others), are incorporating GenAI tools into their platforms. There are many articles and webinars about using these systems with AI capabilities. In the world of legal research and law practice, there seems to be a variety of tasks that can be made more efficient with the use of GenAI. Some of these include document drafting (especially contracts and transactional documents),

---

[12] For some background on GenAI, see University of Chicago Law Library, "Generative AI in Legal Research, Education, and Practice," https://guides.lib.uchicago.edu/AI.

[13] For a list of good resources, see https://www.law.berkeley.edu/library/legal-research/chatgpt/.

document review for litigation, preparing for depositions, exploration of legal experts, legal operations management, and more.[14] Most of what is being touted focuses on U.S. legal research and related legal research platforms. When it comes to jurisdictional comparisons using AI, it's much more focused on comparing U.S. state law and not foreign law.

The developers at vLex, another player in the AI field, have developed "Vincent AI"[15] and have stated that along with 50-state comparative research, "a privacy lawyer who needs to have updates on data-protection laws can examine how it's approached in multiple countries. Finding and analyzing diverse legal standards across jurisdictions—including cross-border considerations—separates good lawyers from great lawyers."[16] The basic vLex database already offers some useful tools not available in other systems, such as the ability to translate words and phrases into various languages for searching and provides machine translations of foreign legal materials.

---

[14] MyCase Blog, Catherine Brock, April 24, 2024, "Legal ChatGPT: Tips, Prompts, and Use Cases," https://www.mycase.com/blog/ai/chatgpt-for-lawyers/. For more in-depth information, see Megan Ma et al., "Whitepaper: Generative AI Legal Landscape 2024," March 6, 2024, https://law.stanford.edu/publications/generative-ai-legal-landscape-2024-2/.

[15] vLex database, https://vlex.com/. See AI Law Librarians, November 30, 2023, "Review: vLex's Vincent AI," https://www.ailawlibrarians.com/2023/11/30/review-vlexs-vincent-ai/.

[16] vLex, "Whitepaper: LLMs for Legal Tasks." February 7, 2024, https://vlex.com/blog/whitepaper-generativeai.

Because vLex contains the primary sources of law for many jurisdictions from around the world, Vincent AI is an interesting development for those who do comparative law research. In a July 2024 webinar, the folks at vLex showed the workflows they have developed using GenAI and utilizing the legal content available from vLex (and not the open web).[17] One of the workflows is called "Compare Jurisdictions" which will allow a researcher to "compare laws and regulations across many jurisdictions at once."[18] Unfortunately, they did not demo this task during the webinar, but I was able to get a trial to test out this workflow. At face value, the ability to do this kind of research quickly and efficiently will be good for the comparative law researcher.

Through this short trial of Vincent AI, I was able to use the "Compare Jurisdictions" workflow. Researchers need to understand that this AI tool is not available without a subscription to vLex and Vincent AI. To date, this is one of the few AI tools really geared for foreign and comparative legal research. During the trial, the following countries were included: US, UK, Spain, Ireland, Chile, Colombia, New Zealand, Mexico, Singapore, and the EU. vLex makes these countries available due to the strength of the content for these jurisdictions. Other

---

[17] vLex, "Developing the Future of Legal AI," https://vimeo.com/985710964.

[18] https://support.vlex.com/features/vincent/compare-jurisdictions.

countries will be added as the tool and content develop.

Comparing jurisdictions is easy to do by starting with a question or statement of what you want to compare. The form states: "In a sentence or two, ask your legal research question in ordinary language. You can change it later if you need to."[19] You then select the jurisdictions you want to compare using the countries available from vLex. For those countries that are part of the EU, you can indicate to include EU law and for those jurisdictions where the content covers federal and state law, you can indicate what you want to include. Currently, only the US, UK, and Mexico offer this option.

I ran searches for questions such as: 1) locate the arbitration laws for these jurisdictions; 2) compare data protection laws; and 3) which countries have climate change laws and provide a list of relevant laws. As with many GenAI tools, the results can take some time to generate, and the information may end up being emailed to the user. When the system is

---

19 Inputs or queries provided by the user in a GenAI tool are often referred to as "prompts." In specialized legal GenAI tools, like Vincent AI, prompting skills are less critical because the system is designed with predefined rules that guide its responses within a narrow scope. In contrast, general purpose GenAI tools, like ChatGPT, rely heavily on prompts to shape the output, since they are designed to handle a broad range of topics and tasks. For more information on the use of prompts, see OpenAI Platform, "Prompt Engineering Guide," https://platform.openai.com/docs/guides/prompt-engineering. See also, Jennifer (Greig) Wondracek, "Introducing AI Prompt Worksheets for the Legal Profession," January 22, 2024, https://www.llrx.com/2024/01/introducing-ai-prompt-worksheets-for-the-legal-profession/.

done, you get a brief answer for each jurisdiction, and you then can link to a complete report. The responses summarize the relevant laws and then link to the primary legal authority (statutes, cases, etc.) on vLex and, if available, secondary sources. In some cases, "exceptions and limitations related to the question" are also noted. For example, for Arbitration in Spain, one of the exceptions/limitations is the following: "Autonomous Communities' Competence: Autonomous Communities do not have the authority to independently regulate arbitration, which is considered a matter of civil procedural law under the exclusive competence of the State."

When you click on a link and go to the legal authority, you can then use the vLex translation feature to get a machine translation of the document in a variety of languages, including English. These translations are not authoritative but may be considered acceptable for research purposes.

If relevant secondary sources are available on vLex, those are included in the full response from Vincent AI, but do not expect a vast array of sources. There may be some journal articles, mostly in the vernacular, but you will not have access to the kinds of commentary and analysis you will find for some jurisdictions on Lexis, Westlaw, or other databases discussed throughout the *Nutshell*.

Practical Law AI (available on Westlaw) was the second legal GenAI I used. You can access this tool from the right side of the screen once you are in Practical Law ("Ask Practical Law AI"). Before you begin using the AI tool, you will see the following caveat: "Ask Practical Law AI uses large language models and can occasionally produce inaccuracies, so it should always be used as part of a research process in connection with additional research where Practical Law resources are checked to fully understand the nuance of the issues and further improve accuracy." This is followed by a box where you can type in your question. I asked the following questions: 1) Please summarize the relevant laws on data protection in the U.S. and Germany, and 2) Please prepare a summary of the arbitration laws for Germany, France, and Spain. The response from the first questions focused mainly on the US and a bit of information about EU law. It links to US Practical Law content but there is no information about German national law on this issue. In response to the second question, I received the following: "I'm sorry, but I cannot answer that question based on trusted Practical Law resources. Please revise your question and try again."

I know that Practical Law contains articles that provide information on both questions. However, this content is in the Practical Law Global section of the database. I then read the "Ask How Practical Law AI works" and saw the description of what's searched: "Ask Practical Law AI uses large language models [LLMs]—a type of generative AI—and focuses the models on the text of Practical Law resources to improve accuracy. Practical Law resources are referenced in the responses with the actual language from the resources, and links are included to read the full Practical Law documents."[20] It seems that Practical Law AI does not include Practical Law Global content in its LLMs. Westlaw confirmed that the global content is not included. Therefore, currently, this AI tool does not provide much use for foreign and comparative law research. However, I do appreciate this statement from Westlaw: "Use it to accelerate thorough research. Don't use it as a replacement for thorough research." Good words to live by.

By the way, if you do want to use Practical Law for foreign and comparative law research, you can find many useful articles on a variety of topics and you can also use the "Country Q&A Comparison Tool." See Chapter 3 of the *Nutshell* for more information.

I also tried the Lexis+ AI Assistant since it offers the "Practical Guidance" materials which does include content for foreign jurisdictions, somewhat like Practical Law Global from Westlaw. I used the same questions noted above for Westlaw's AI tool and did not get any information regarding other countries. If you look at the "Select Jurisdiction" option, you will see that it only covers US law. I did note this message at the end of the results about US law: "AI-generated content should be reviewed for accuracy."

Finally, I want to bring your attention to another legal AI tool from Jus Mundi[21] called "Jus AI

---

[20] This information is available when you access "Ask Practical Law AI" once you sign on to the system.

[21] https://jusmundi.com/en (subscription database).

Assistant." Jus Mundi is an international law and arbitration database, and the search engine uses AI and machine learning to enhance the quality of the search results.[22] The database focuses on treaties, arbitration cases and awards, rules, Jus Mundi publications, and "libraries" of publications from other publishers (OUP, Brill, ICC). The primary focus of the content is international commercial arbitration and investment disputes. Some more general treaties are also included, like the Vienna Convention on the Law of Treaties (VCLT).

Unfortunately, I was not able to try out the "Jus AI Assistant" but there is a YouTube video that does a good job explaining how this AI tool works.[23] Briefly, this AI tool operates much in the same way as the other tools I mentioned above. You ask the system a question or a series of questions (starting a "conversation") and the system searches the Jus Mundi collection of specialized content to create the answer. Summaries are provided with footnotes to the sources from the Jus Mundi database. Currently, there is a "Jus AI Acceleration Program" in progress and law firms that practice international commercial arbitration and investment arbitration are learning to use Jus AI Assistant.[24] There are also plans to allow subscribers, maybe just law firms, to upload confidential documents for translation and analysis,

---

[22] https://help.jusmundi.com/en/articles/4396999-about-jus-mundi-search-engine.

[23] Jus Mundi, "Jus AI Acceleration Program," Webinar, https://www.youtube.com/watch?v=hC7JNKJRpn0.

[24] Daily Jus, Legal Tech & AI blog, https://dailyjus.com/category/legal-tech.

in addition to the content already available on the database. Note that the collection of documents (treaties, cases, etc.) are in many different languages, but you can ask your question in any language and retrieve sources in other languages. vLex does this as well.

Overall, I think these examples offer some valid reasons for using GenAI tools in legal research. Legal AI tools, like the ones noted above, certainly can aid international and comparative law research by improving efficiency, expanding the scope of what the researcher can accomplish, and save time.[25] However, I do have some concerns:

- Verify what is found by any legal GenAI tool. vLex refers to this as "trust but verify." I say verify and then trust. "Lawyers will still need to read and cite check any case that is recommended using a commercial Generative AI product designed for the legal market."[26] Both vLex and Jus AI Assistant link to the legal authorities cited in the responses and this makes verifying easier.
- The translations of primary sources are automated and are not done by a lawyer or

[25] For more information, see vLex, "Whitepaper: LLMs for Legal Tasks," February 7, 2024, https://vlex.com/blog/whitepaper-generativeai.

[26] Dewey B Strategic, Jean O'Grady, July 1, 2024, "Generative AI Risk in Legal Research: Is the Fault in the Technology or in Ourselves? Answer is Both," https://www.deweybstrategic.com/2024/07/generative-ai-risk-in-legal-research-is-the-fault-in-the-technology-or-in-ourselves-answer-is-both.html.

legal translator with the necessary language abilities and expertise in the legal system(s) at issue. These translations are useful for the researcher but are not authoritative.

- Most responses do not contain information on the differences in legal systems, civil law vs. common law. You need to understand the legal systems you are researching and how each jurisdiction operates. Without this knowledge, you may make assumptions about the hierarchy of law and what law is most relevant.
- Be sure to understand the scope of the content being compared. You need to know the coverage for the collection of law (dates covered and if all sources of law are included) and what secondary sources are included in the database.
- Be aware of "hallucinations," AI generated false or misleading information (more limited in a closed system, like Vincent AI).[27]
- Other concerns and risks associated with AI in legal research.[28]

---

27 Varun Magesh et al., "Hallucination-Free? Assessing the Reliability of Leading AI Legal Research Tools," https://dho.stanford.edu/wp-content/uploads/Legal_RAG_Hallucinations.pdf.

28 See Dewey B Strategic, Jean O'Grady, July 1, 2024, "Generative AI Risk in Legal Research: Is the Fault in the Technology or in Ourselves? Answer is Both," https://www.deweybstrategic.com/2024/07/generative-ai-risk-in-legal-research-is-the-fault-in-the-technology-or-in-ourselves-answer-is-both.html.

While my exploration of legal AI tools was brief, I do see some future potential uses for using AI for international and foreign legal research:

- Provide an efficient method for comparing the law of different jurisdictions.
- Ability to find common clauses in international documents, like treaties and agreements, to further develop general principles of law.
- Quickly analyze and summarize international case law for general principles and customary international law.
- Find commentators ("publicists" in the international law context) for various subjects.
- Summarize secondary sources to find needed backup with citations to primary law.
- Automated translations of user-created documents.
- Creating forms and other transactional documents in other languages.

GenAI tools do offer advantages by making some of the legal research processes faster and more efficient. Remember that while legal AI tools can summarize, synthesize, and highlight legal authorities and other sources, many of the skills you need for doing effective legal research also apply when using these tools.

Since the space where technology and legal research is evolving quickly, I suggest monitoring sources that cover these changes. A few sources for staying ahead of the curve are listed in Chapter 13 under "legal technology blogs." To learn more about the ever-growing area of legal GenAI tools, see Kristie Chamorro's "Generative AI Resources" webpage on the Berkeley Law Library website.[29] This list is curated and updated to help researchers better understand how to use these tools in legal research and the impact of GenAI in law schools and the legal profession.

---

[29] https://www.law.berkeley.edu/library/legal-research/chatgpt/.

APPENDIX A

COMPREHENSIVE LIST OF SOURCES

This is a (mostly) comprehensive list of the sources cited throughout this *Nutshell*, including print sources, subscription databases, and freely available sources and websites. All references to Lexis and Westlaw are basic and do not specify any name changes or branding.

For access to subscription databases, check with a friendly reference librarian at your law library.

3 Geeks and a Law Blog, https://www.geeklawblog.com/.

Abkürzungsverzeichnis der Rechtssprache (10th ed. 2021).

African Child Rights Cases, https://www.acerwc.africa/en/resources/case-law-database.

African Human Rights Case Law Analyser, https://caselaw.ihrda.org/.

African Legal Information Institute, https://africanlii.org/.

African Yearbook of International Law: Annuaire Africain de Droit International (1994–). Available on Brill Online and HeinOnline (subscription databases).

AI Law Librarians, November 30, 2023, "Review: vLex's Vincent AI," https://www.

ailawlibrarians.com/2023/11/30/review-vlexs-vincent-ai/.

Jennifer Allison, "Foreign Law—Subject Law Collections on the Web," https://www.nyulawglobal.org/globalex/foreign_collections1.html.

ALR International: Annotations and Cases (2010–). Available on Westlaw.

American Journal of Comparative Law (1952–). Available on HeinOnline, JSTOR, and other subscription databases.

American Journal of International Law (1907–). Available on HeinOnline, JSTOR, and other subscription databases.

Amnesty International Research, https://www.amnesty.org/en/latest/research/.

Maureen Ratynski Andersen, "Where to Begin . . . When You Don't Know How to Start: Tips for Researching U.N. Legal Materials," 31 *Int'l J. Legal Info.* 264 (2003). Available on HeinOnline (subscription database).

Annotated Leading Cases of International Criminal Tribunals (1999–), https://www.annotatedleadingcases.com/ (subscription database).

Annuaire Français de Droit International (1955–).

John G. Apple & Robert P. Deyling, *A Primer on the Civil-Law System* (1995), https://www.

govinfo.gov/app/details/GOVPUB-JU13-PURL-LPS55055.

Archbold International Criminal Courts: Practice, Procedure and Evidence (5th ed. 2018).

Asian Legal Information Institute (AsianLII), http://www.asianlii.org/.

Asia-Pacific Journal of Ocean Law and Policy (2016–). Available on Brill Online (subscription database).

Asian Yearbook of International Law (1993–). Available on HeinOnline (subscription database).

ASIL Insights, https://www.asil.org/insights.

Associations Unlimited (formerly known as the *Encyclopedia of Associations: International Organizations* (1989–)), https://www.gale.com/c/associations-unlimited (subscription database).

Australasian Legal Information Institute (AustLII), https://www.austlii.edu.au/.

Australia's Department of Foreign Affairs and Trade, https://www.dfat.gov.au/.

Australian Guide to Legal Citation (4th ed. 2018), https://law.unimelb.edu.au/mulr/aglc/about.

Australian Treaties Library, https://www.austlii.edu.au/au/other/dfat/.

Australian Yearbook of International Law (1966–). Available on HeinOnline (subscription database).

Francisco Avalos, *Avalos Legal Glossary / Dictionary Translator and Other Related Fields of Study: English / Spanish Spanish / English* (2018).

BabelFish Translator, https://www.babelfish.com/.

"Basic & Background Sources for International and Foreign Legal Research," Berkeley Law Library, https://libguides.law.berkeley.edu/c.php?g=326623.

Bepress Legal Repository, http://law.bepress.com/.

Berkeley Law Scholarship Repository, https://www.law.berkeley.edu/library/ir/.

Robert C. Berring et al., *How to Find the Law* (12th ed. 2005).

Bing Translator, https://www.bing.com/translator.

Bloomberg Law, https://www.bloomberglaw.com/ (subscription database).

The Bluebook: A Uniform Style of Citations (21st ed. 2020). Available at https://www.legalbluebook.com/ (subscription database). Table 2 of *The Bluebook* has moved online, https://www.legalbluebook.com/bluebook/v21/tables/t2-foreign-jurisdictions. Access to this table is free even though the electronic version of *The Bluebook* is by subscription.

Boleslaw A. Boczek, *International Law: A Dictionary* (2005).

Box, https://www.box.com/home.

Curtis Bradley, Jack Goldsmith & Oona Hathaway, "Congress Mandates Sweeping Transparency Reforms for International Agreements" (12/23/2022), https://www.lawfaremedia.org/article/congress-mandates-sweeping-transparency-reforms-international-agreements.

Curtis Bradley, Jack Goldsmith & Oona Hathaway, "The Rise of Nonbinding International Agreements: An Empirical, Comparative, and Normative Analysis," 90 *Univ. Chicago L. Rev.* 1281, 1286 (2023), https://lawreview.uchicago.edu/print-archive/rise-nonbinding-international-agreements-empirical-comparative-and-normative-analysis.

The Brainyacts, https://thebrainyacts.beehiiv.com/.

British and Irish Legal Information Institute (BAILII), https://www.bailii.org/.

Ian Brownlie, *Principles of Public International Law* (9th ed. 2019).

Thomas Buergenthal & Sean Murphy, *Public International Law in a Nutshell* (6th ed. 2019).

Available on West Academic (subscription database).

Cadwalader, *Digest of the Published Opinions of the Attorneys-General and of the Leading Decisions of the Federal Courts, with Reference to International Law, Treaties, and Kindred Subjects* (1877). Available on HeinOnline (subscription database).

The Cambridge Companion to International Organizations Law (Jan Klabbers ed., 2022).

The Cambridge Handbook of Comparative Law (Mathias Siems & Po Jen Yap., eds., 2024).

Cambridge Law Reports, https://www.cambridge.org/core/publications/collections/cambridge-law-reports-collection (subscription database).

Cambridge University Press, https://www.cambridge.org/core (subscription database).

Canada Legal Information Institute (CanLII), https://www.canlii.org.

Canadian Guide to Uniform Legal Citation = Manuel Canadien de la Référence Juridique (10th ed. 2023). Available on Westlaw Canada.

Cardiff Index to Legal Abbreviations, https://www.legalabbrevs.cardiff.ac.uk/.

Case Law on UNCITRAL Texts (CLOUT), https://uncitral.un.org/en/case_law.

Kristie Chamorro, "Generative AI Resources," https://www.law.berkeley.edu/library/legal-research/chatgpt/.

Chemical Weapons Convention, OPCW Legislation Compendium, https://www.opcw.org/resources/national-implementation/legislation-compendium.

Bin Cheng, *General Principles of Law, as applied by International Courts and Tribunals* (1953).

Daniel C.K. Chow et al., *The Legal System of the People's Republic of China in a Nutshell* (4th ed. 2023).

CIS Legislation, https://cis-legislation.com/ (subscription database).

Andrew Clapman, *Brierly's Law of Nations: An Introduction to the International Law of Peace* (7th ed. 2012).

CODICES Database (Council of Europe), https://codices.coe.int/codices/documents/welcome.

Collected Course of the Hague Academy of International Law = Recueil des Cours de l'Académie de la Haye en ligne (1923–). Available on HeinOnline and Brill Online (subscription databases).

"Collected Travaux Préparatoires," Yale Law Library, https://library.law.yale.edu/research-guides/collected-travaux-preparatoires.

Company Law in Europe (1992–).

Comparative Law Prof Blog, http://lawprofessors.typepad.com/comparative_law/.

Competition Policy International, https://www.pymnts.com/cpi (subscription database).

Benedetto Conforti, *The Law and Practice of the United Nations* (5th rev. ed. 2016).

Congress.gov, Treaty Documents, https://www.congress.gov/treaties.

Consolidated Treaty Series (1969–1981). Available on Oxford Historical Treaties, https://opil.ouplaw.com/home/OHT (subscription database).

Constitute Project, https://www.constituteproject.org/.

Contemporary Women's Issues, https://www.gale.com/c/onefile-contemporary-womens-issues (subscription database).

Council of Europe, https://www.coe.int/en/.

Council of Europe, *European Conventions and Agreements* (1971–1999).

Council of Europe, *European Treaty Series* (1949–), https://www.coe.int/en/web/conventions/full-list.

"Country by Country Guide to Foreign Legal Research," Yale Law Library, https://library.law.yale.edu/research-guides/country-country-guide-foreign-legal-research.

Court of Justice of the European Union (CURIA), https://curia.europa.eu/jcms/jcms/j_6/en/.

Criminal Law Library Blog, August 4, 2024, "Google's Increasing Selectivity: Effects on Information Access and Diversity," https://www.criminallawlibraryblog.com/googles-increasing-selectivity-effects-on-information-access-and-diversity/.

Cumulative Digest of United States Practice in International Law (1981–). Available at https://www.state.gov/digest-of-united-states-practice-in-international-law/.

Current Index to Legal Periodicals (CILP). Available on HeinOnline (subscription database).

Current Treaty Index, (I. Kavass & A. Sprudzs, eds., 1982–). Available on HeinOnline (subscription database).

Dahl's French-English Law Dictionary (3rd ed. 2007).

Dahl's Spanish-English Law Dictionary (6th ed. 2015).

Data Protection Laws of the World (1988–).

Decisions of the Korean Constitutional Court (2000–), https://english.ccourt.go.kr/site/eng/

main.do and https://library.ccourt.go.kr/en/#/about/pub/case.

Dec.Nat., Association of the Councils of State and Supreme Administrative Jurisdictions (ACA) of the European Union (EU), https://www.aca-europe.eu/index.php/en/dec-nat-en.

DeepL, https://www.deepl.com/ko/translator.

Eileen Denza, *Diplomatic Law: A Commentary on the Vienna Convention on Diplomatic Relations* (4th ed. 2016).

Department of State Bulletin (1939–1989) and *Dispatch* (1990–1999). Available on Hathitrust, https://catalog.hathitrust.org/Record/000598610 and HeinOnline, Law Journal Library (subscription database).

Dewey B Strategic, https://www.deweybstrategic.com/.

Dewey B Strategic, Jean O'Grady, July 1, 2024, "Generative AI Risk in Legal Research: Is the Fault in the Technology or in Ourselves? Answer is Both," https://www.deweybstrategic.com/2024/07/generative-ai-risk-in-legal-research-is-the-fault-in-the-technology-or-in-ourselves-answer-is-both.html

Digest of Commercial Laws of the World (1998–). Available on Westlaw.

Digest of United States Practice in International Law (1973–1980; 2001–), https://www.state.gov/digest-of-united-states-practice-in-international-law/. Available on HeinOnline (subscription database).

Digital Public Library of America, https://dp.la/.

DipLawMatic Dialogues, https://fcilsis.wordpress.com/.

Directory of Open Access Journals (DOAJ), https://doaj.org/.

"Dockets and Court Documents by Country," UCLA Law Library, https://libguides.law.ucla.edu/internationaldockets.

Curtis F.J. Doebbler, *Dictionary of Public International Law* (2018).

DOI Foundation, https://www.doi.org.

Dropbox, https://www.dropbox.com/.

e-Bulletin on Constitutional Case-Law (1993–), https://www.venice.coe.int/WebForms/pages/?p=02_02_Bulletins.

Early English Books Online, https://proquest.libguides.com/eebopqp/content (subscription database).

East European Case Reporter of Constitutional Law (1994–).

EconLit, https://proquest.libguides.com/econlit (subscription database).

Frederic Eggermont & Stafaan Smis, *Research Guide to Instruments of European Regional Organizations* (2015).

EJIL: The Podcast!, European Journal of International Law, https://www.ejiltalk.org/ejil-the-podcast-page/.

Elgar Encyclopedia of Comparative Law (Jan M. Smits et al., eds., 2023–). Available on Elgaronline (subscription database). There are earlier versions of this source issued as single volume treatises. The 2023 database is much more comprehensive.

Elgaronline, https://www.elgaronline.com/ (subscription database).

Elgaronline Journals, https://www.elgaronline.com/page/82 (subscription database).

Encyclopedia of European Union Law (1996–).

Encyclopedia of Private International Law (2017—), https://www.elgaronline.com/ (subscription database).

Encyclopedia of Public International Law (1981–1990; 1992–1998, 2012). Available at https://opil.ouplaw.com/home/EPIL (subscription database). See entry for *Max Planck Encyclopedias of International Law* below.

EndNote, https://endnote.com/ (subscription database). Check with your library to see if your institution offers access to EndNote.

ESCR-Net Caselaw Database, https://www.escr-net.org/caselaw.

Estonian Legislation in English, https://www.riigiteataja.ee/en/.

Ethnic NewsWatch, https://proquest.libguides.com/diversitycollection (subscription database).

EUR-Lex (EU law), https://eur-lex.europa.eu/homepage.html?locale=en.

Europa World Database (formerly *The Europa Directory of International Organizations* (1999–)), https://www.europaworld.com (subscription database).

European Convention on Human Rights (ECHR), https://www.coe.int/en/web/conventions/.

European Court of Human Rights (ECtHR), https://www.echr.coe.int/home.

European Court of Human Rights, HUDOC, https://www.echr.coe.int/hudoc-database.

European Court of Human Rights, Knowledge Sharing (ECHR-KS) Platform, https://www.echr.coe.int/knowledge-sharing#.

European Court of Justice, https://curia.europa.eu/jcms/jcms/Jo1_6308/.

European Court of Justice, *European Court Reports* (1990–).

European Court of Justice, *Reports of Cases before the Court* (1959–1989).

European Current Law: Monthly Digest (1992–).

European Current Law Year Book (1993–).

European e-Justice Portal, https://e-justice.europa.eu/home.do?action=home.

European Law Blog: News and Comments on EU Law, https://europeanlawblog.eu/.

"European Union—A Guide to Tracing Working Documents," GlobaLex, https://www.nyulawglobal.org/globalex/European_Union_Travaux_Preparatoires1.html.

European Union, Court of Auditors, https://www.eca.europa.eu/en.

European Union, European Commission, https://commission.europa.eu/index_en.

European Union, European Commission, (COM) Documents, https://ec.europa.eu/transparency/documents-register/ and https://eur-lex.europa.eu/collection/eu-law/pre-acts.html.

European Union, European Council and the Council of the European Union, https://www.consilium.europa.eu/en/.

European Union, European Economic and Social Committee, https://www.eesc.europa.eu/en.

European Union, European Parliament, https://www.europarl.europa.eu/portal/en.

European Union Gateway (formerly known as Europa), https://european-union.europa.eu/index_en.

European Union, Institutions and Bodies, https://european-union.europa.eu/institutions-law-budget/institutions-and-bodies/search-all-eu-institutions-and-bodies_en.

"European Union Law: Brexit," Bodleian Library Research Guide (Oxford University), https://libguides.bodleian.ox.ac.uk/c.php?g=422926&p=4678442.

European Union Law Guide (2011—). Available on Westlaw.

"European Union Legal Materials: An Infrequent User's Guide," GlobaLex, https://www.nyulawglobal.org/globalex/European_Union1.html.

European Union, N-Lex, https://n-lex.europa.eu/n-lex/index?lang=en.

European Union Treaties, https://eur-lex.europa.eu/collection/eu-law/treaties/treaties-force.html.

Evernote, https://evernote.com/.

The Evolution of EU Law (Paul Craig & Gráinne de Búrca, eds., 3rd ed. 2021).

Extraordinary Chambers in the Courts of Cambodia (ECCC), https://www.eccc.gov.kh/en.

FinLex, https://www.finlex.fi/en/.

Firstsearch, https://help.oclc.org/Discovery_and_Reference/FirstSearch/FirstSearch_databases (subscription database).

Flare Index to Treaties, https://resources.ials.sas.ac.uk/digital/ials-digital-resources/flare-index-treaties.

Ralph Folsom, *European Union Law including Brexit and Beyond in a Nutshell* (10th ed. 2021). Available on West Academic (subscription database).

Food and Agriculture Organization (FAO), *Code of Conduct for Responsible Fisheries* (1995).

Food and Agriculture Organization (FAO), FAOLEX, https://www.fao.org/faolex/en.

Forced Migration Current Awareness Blog, https://fm-cab.blogspot.com/.

Foreign Law Guide, https://referenceworks.brill.com/display/db/flg (subscription database).

Foreign Law Translations (France, Germany, Austria, Israel), https://law.utexas.edu/transnational/foreign-law-translations/.

Foreign Relations of the United States (1861–), https://history.state.gov/historicaldocuments. Available on HeinOnline (subscription database).

Nigel Foster, *Foster on EU Law* (8th ed. 2021).

James R. Fox, *Dictionary of International and Comparative Law* (3rd ed. 2003).

Free Access to Law Movement (FALM), http://www.falm.info/.

Freedom of Information Database (freedominfo.org), https://www.freedominfo.org/regions/.

"Frequently-Cited Treaties & Other International Instruments," University of Minnesota Law Library, https://libguides.law.umn.edu/frequentlycitedtreaties.

Julie Roberts Furgerson, *Prince's Dictionary of Legal Abbreviations: A Reference Guide for Attorneys, Legal Secretaries, Paralegals, and Law Students* (10th ed. 2021).

Gallica, https://gallica.bnf.fr/.

GATT Digital Library, 1947–1994, https://exhibits.stanford.edu/gatt.

GATT Documents, World Trade Organization (WTO), https://www.wto.org/english/docs_e/gattdocs_e.htm.

GenderWatch, https://proquest.libguides.com/diversitycollection (subscription database).

General Principles and the Coherence of International Law (2019). Available on Brill Online (subscription database).

General Principles of Law in the Decisions of International Criminal Courts and Tribunals

(2008). Available on Brill Online (subscription database).

General Principles of Law Recognized by Civilized Nations (1922–2018): The Evolution of the Third Source of International Law Through the Jurisprudence of the Permanent Court of International Justice and the International Court of Justice (2020).

"Generative AI in Legal Research, Education, and Practice," University of Chicago Law Library, https://guides.lib.uchicago.edu/AI.

Mary W. George, *The Elements of Library Research* (2008).

German Law on the Internet (Gesetze im Internet), https://www.gesetze-im-internet.de/Teilliste_translations.html.

German Law Journal, https://www.germanlawjournal.com/.

German Practice in International Law (Stefan Talmon ed., 2022–).

German Yearbook of International Law (1948–). Available on HeinOnline (subscription database).

Germany's Auswärtiges Amt [Federal Foreign Office], https://www.auswaertiges-amt.de/de/.

Gesetze im Internet (German Law on the Internet), https://www.gesetze-im-internet.de/Teilliste_translations.html.

María-Teresa Gil-Bazo, "Asylum as a General Principle of International Law," 27 *Int'l J Refugee Law* 3 (2015), https://doi.org/10.1093/ijrl/eeu062.

H. Patrick Glen, *Legal Traditions of the World* (5th ed. 2014).

Mary Ann Glendon, *Comparative Legal Traditions in a Nutshell* (4th ed. 2016). Available on West Academic (subscription database).

Global Database on Violence Against Women (UN Women), https://evaw-global-database.unwomen.org/en.

Globalex, https://nyulawglobal.org/globalex/.

Global Freedom of Expression, https://globalfreedomofexpression.columbia.edu.

Global Gender Equality Constitutional Database, https://constitutions.unwomen.org/en.

Global Health and Human Rights Database, https://www.globalhealthrights.org/.

Global Journal of Comparative Law (2012–). Available on Brill Online and HeinOnline (subscription databases).

Global Legal Monitor, https://www.loc.gov/collections/global-legal-monitor/about-this-collection/.

Global Regulation, https://www.global-regulation.com/ (subscription database).

Goettingen Journal of International Law, https://www.gojil.eu/.

L.M. Goodrich et al., *Charter of the United Nations: Commentary and Documents* (3rd ed. 1969).

Google Advanced Search, https://www.google.com/advanced_search.

Google Books, https://books.google.com.

Google Drive, https://www.google.com/drive/.

"Google Research Made Easy," UC Berkeley Library, https://guides.lib.berkeley.edu/GoogleTips.

Google Scholar, https://scholar.google.com.

Google Scholar, Advanced Search, https://scholar.google.com/#d=gs_asd&t=1721074891137.

Google Translate, https://translate.google.com.

Grotius Centre Working Paper Series, https://www.universiteitleiden.nl/en/law/institute-of-public-law/grotius-centre/research/grotius-centre-working-paper-serie.

Guide to Foreign and International Legal Citations (2nd ed. 2009).

Guide to International Legal Research (annual). Available on Lexis.

"Guide to Law Online: Nations of the World," Law Library of Congress, https://guides.loc.gov/nations-world.

Green Haywood Hackworth, *Digest of International Law* (1940–1944). Available on HeinOnline (subscription database).

Hague Conventions on Private International Law, https://www.hcch.net/en/instruments/conventions.

Handbook on Legal Cultures: A Selection of the World's Legal Cultures (Sören Koch & Marius Mikkel Kjølstad, eds., 2023).

Alexandra R. Harrington, *International Organizations and the Law* (2nd ed. 2023).

Oona A. Hathaway, Curtis A. Bradley & Jack L. Goldsmith, "The Failed Transparency Regime for Executive Agreements: An Empirical and Normative Analysis," 134 *Harv. L. Rev.* 629, 632 (2020), https://harvardlawreview.org/print/vol-134/the-failed-transparency-regime-for-executive-agreements/.

HeinOnline, https://heinonline.org/ (subscription database). HeinOnline has many relevant international and foreign law collections/libraries, including the following:

English Reports

Foreign & International Law Resources Database

Foreign Relations of the United States

Hague Academy Collected Courses Online/ Recueil des cours en ligne

Harvard Research in International Law

History of International Law

Index to Foreign Legal Periodicals (IFLP)

International & Non-U.S. Law Journals

Israel Law Reports

Multinational Sources Compared

Legal Classics: International Law

United Nations Law Collection

U.S. Treaty and Agreements Library

World Constitutions Illustrated

World Treaty Library

World Trials Library

Hong Kong, Bilingual Laws Information System https://www.elegislation.gov.hk.

Hong Kong Legal Information Institute (HKLII), https://www.hklii.org/.

HUDOC (Council of Europe), https://hudoc.echr.coe.int/eng.

IATE ("Inter-Active Terminology for Europe"), https://iate.europa.eu/home.

*ICSID Reports: Reports of Cases Decided under the Convention on the Settlement of Investment Disputes between States and Nationals of Other States, **1965*** (1993–).

IMF eLibrary, https://www.elibrary.imf.org/.

In Custodia Legis, https://blogs.loc.gov/law/.

Index to Foreign Legal Periodicals (IFLP), available on HeinOnline (subscription database).

Index to Legal Periodicals and Books (ILP), https://www.ebsco.com/products/research-databases/index-legal-periodicals-books (subscription database).

Indian Practice of International Law: Global Norms and their Domestic Enforcement (Siddhartha Misra ed., 2024).

Information Systems of International Inter-Governmental Organizations: A Reference Guide (1998).

Institute for Transnational Law, University of Texas at Austin Law School, https://law.utexas.edu/transnational/foreign-law-translations/.

Inter-American Court of Human Rights (IACtHR), https://www.corteidh.or.cr/index.cfm?lang=en.

Inter-American Court of Human Rights Project, https://iachr.lls.edu/database.

"International Arbitration & Litigation," Berkeley Law Library, https://libguides.law.berkeley.edu/c.php?g=326736.

International Arbitration Treaties (3rd ed. 2010–), https://arbitrationlaw.com/ (subscription database).

International Bureau of Fiscal Documentation (IBFD) Tax Research Platform, https://www.ibfd.org/ (subscription database).

International Centre for Settlement of Investment Disputes (ICSID), https://icsid.worldbank.org/en/.

International Centre for Settlement of Investment Disputes (ICSID), Case Database, https://icsid.worldbank.org/cases/case-database.

International Citation Manual, https://apps.law.wustl.edu/gslr/icm.html.

International Citator and Research Guide: The Greenbook (2018–).

International Committee of the Red Cross (ICRC), https://www.icrc.org/en.

International Committee of the Red Cross, Customary International Humanitarian Law, https://ihl-databases.icrc.org/en/customary-ihl.

International Committee of the Red Cross, International Humanitarian Law Bibliography, https://www.icrc.org/en/document/international-humanitarian-law-bibliography.

International Committee of the Red Cross, National Implementation of International Humanitarian Law, https://ihl-databases.icrc.org/en/national-practice/national-implementation-of-ihl.

International Comparative Legal Guides (ICLG), https://iclg.com/ (subscription database, some content is freely available).

International Court of Justice, https://www.icj-cij.org/home.

International Court of Justice Statute, Article 38, https://www.icj-cij.org/statute.

"International Courts and Tribunals," Harvard Law Library, https://guides.library.harvard.edu/law/internationalcourts.

International Courts and Tribunals Series (Oxford University Press), https://global.oup.com/academic/content/series/i/international-courts-and-tribunals-series-icts/?cc=us&lang=en&.

International Crimes Database (ICD), https://www.internationalcrimesdatabase.org/.

International Criminal Court (ICC), https://www.icc-cpi.int/.

International Criminal Court, ICC Case Law Database, https://www.legal-tools.org/cld.

International Criminal Court, ICC Legal Tools Database, https://www.legal-tools.org/.

International Criminal Tribunal for Rwanda (ICTR), https://unictr.irmct.org/.

International Criminal Tribunal for the Former Yugoslavia (ICTY), https://www.icty.org/.

International Economic Law and Policy Blog, https://worldtradelaw.typepad.com/.

International Encyclopaedia of Laws, https://www.kluwerlawonline.com/ (subscription database).

International Enforcement Law Reporter (1985–), http://www.ielr.com/ (subscription database).

"International Human Rights," Berkeley Law Library, https://libguides.law.berkeley.edu/c.php?g=326748.

International Journal of Refugee Law (1989–). Available on Oxford Journals and HeinOnline (subscription databases).

International Labour Law Reports (1978–).

International Labour Organizations (ILO), NATLEX, https://natlex.ilo.org/dyn/natlex2/r/natlex/fe/home.

International Law Behind the Headlines, ASIL, https://www.asil.org/podcast.

International Law Commission, https://legal.un.org/ilc/texts/texts.shtml.

International Law in Brief, https://www.asil.org/ilib.

International Law Reporter, https://ilreports.blogspot.com/.

International Law Reports (1919–). Available on vLex and Cambridge Law Reports (subscription databases).

International Residual Mechanism for Criminal Tribunals (IRMCT), https://www.irmct.org/en.

International Residual Mechanism for Criminal Tribunals, Case Law Database, https://cld.irmct.org/.

International Securities Regulation (2012–). Available on Westlaw.

International Tribunal for the Law of the Sea (ITLOS), https://www.itlos.org/.

Internet Archives, Million Book Project, https://archive.org/details/millionbooks.

IntLawGrrls, https://ilg2.org.

Introduction to Turkish Law (Tŭgrul Ansay & Don Wallace, Jr., eds., 7th ed. 2020).

Investment Laws of the World (1972–).

Investment Promotion and Protection Treaties (1983–).

Investment Treaty Arbitration (italaw), https://www.italaw.com/.

Investor-State LawGuide, https://new.investorstatelawguide.com/ (subscription database).

Japanese Annual of International Law (1957–2007). Continued by the *Japanese Yearbook of International Law* (2009–). Available on HeinOnline (subscription database).

Japanese Law Translation, https://www.japaneselawtranslation.go.jp/.

Philip C. Jessup, *Transnational Law* (1956).

Stellina Jolly & Nafees Ahmad, *Climate Refugees in South Asia: Protection Under International Legal Standards and State Practices in South Asia* (2019).

Journal of Civil Law Studies, https://digitalcommons.law.lsu.edu/jcls/.

Journal of Comparative Law in Africa (2014–).

Journal of International Dispute Settlement (2010–), https://academic.oup.com/jids (subscription database).

Journal on the Use of Force and International Law (2014–), https://www.tandfonline.com/journals/rjuf20 (subscription database).

JSTOR, https://www.jstor.org/ (subscription database).

Jumpstart Your Foreign, Comparative, and International Research, https://www.aallnet.org/fcilsis/resources-publications/research-resources/jumpstart/.

Juricaf, https://juricaf.org/.

JuriGlobe-World Legal Systems, https://www.juriglobe.ca/eng/.

Juris-M, https://juris-m.github.io.

Jus Cogens: The International Law Podcast, https://podcasters.spotify.com/pod/show/jus-cogens-podcast.

Jus Mundi, https://jusmundi.com/en (subscription database).

Jus Mundi, Daily Jus, Legal Tech & AI blog, https://dailyjus.com/category/legal-tech.

Jus Mundi, "Jus AI Acceleration Program," Webinar, https://www.youtube.com/watch?v=hC7JNKJRpn0.

Just Security, https://www.justsecurity.org/.

Igor I. Kavass, *World Dictionary of Legal Abbreviations* (1991–).

Igor I. Kavass, *A Guide to the United States Treaties in Force: Current Treaty Action Supplement* (1982–). Available on HeinOnline (subscription database).

Igor I. Kavass & A. Sprudzs, *A Guide to the United States Treaties in Force* (1982–). Available on HeinOnline (subscription database).

Jan Klabbers, *International Organizations* (2005).

Kluwer Arbitration, https://www.kluwerarbitration.com (subscription database).

Kluwer Arbitration Blog, https://arbitrationblog.kluwerarbitration.com/.

Kluwer IP, https://www.kluweriplaw.com/ (subscription database).

Robert Kolb, *The Elgar Companion to the International Court of Justice* (2014).

Robert Kolb, *The Law of Treaties: An Introduction* (2nd ed. 2023).

Korean Journal of International and Comparative Law (2013–), Available on Brill Online (subscription database).

LawFare Blog, https://www.lawfaremedia.org/.

Law Library of Congress, Foreign Legal Gazettes, https://loc.maps.arcgis.com/apps/dashboards/72089675f5e845f99d8e6c12e892b96a#p1=Complete.

Law Library of Congress, Legal Reports, https://www.loc.gov/collections/publications-of-the-law-library-of-congress/about-this-collection/.

The Law & Practice of International Courts and Tribunals (2002–). Available on Brill Online (subscription database).

Law Reports of the Commonwealth (1994–).

Law Review Commons, https://lawreview commons.com/.

LawSites, https://www.lawnext.com/.

League of Nations Treaty Series (1920–1946), https://treaties.un.org/Pages/Content.aspx?path =DB/LoNOnline/pageIntro_en.xml. Available on HeinOnline (subscription database).

Amanda Lee, May 23, 2024, "The Best AI Translators for Legal Translations in 2024," https://beringlab.com/2024/05/23/the-best-ai-translators-for-legal-translations-in-2024/.

Legal History, https://legalhistoryblog.blogspot. com/.

"Legal Interpreting and Translating: Online Resources," University of Iowa Law Library, https://libguides.law.uiowa.edu/c.php?g= 103196&p=669077.

Legal Journals Index (LJI). Available on Westlaw.

Legal Resource Index (LRI). Available on Lexis, Westlaw, and on the web as LegalTrac, https://www.gale.com/c/onefile-legaltrac (subscription database).

Legal Scholarship Network (LSN), https://www. ssrn.com/index.cfm/en/lsn/.

Legifrance, https://www.legifrance.gouv.fr/.

Monroe Leigh et al., *National Treaty Law and Practice: Canada, Egypt, Israel, Mexico, Russia, South Africa* (2003).

Lexis, https://www.lexisnexis.com/en-us/products/lexis.page (subscription database).

Lexology, Panoramic (formerly Getting the Deal Through), https://www.lexology.com (subscription database) and Bloomberg Law.

Lyonette Louis-Jacques, "The INT-LAW Email Discussion List Migrates to Google Groups," Slaw, https://www.slaw.ca/2018/03/13/the-int-law-email-discussion-list-migrates-to-google-groups/.

Lovdata in English (Norway), https://lovdata.no/info/information_in_english.

Megan Ma et al., "White Paper: Generative AI Legal Landscape 2024," March 6, 2024, https://law.stanford.edu/publications/generative-ai-legal-landscape-2024-2/.

Peter Maggs et al., *Law and Legal System of the Russian Federation* (7th ed. 2020).

The Making of Modern Law, https://www.gale.com/primary-sources/making-of-modern-law (subscription database).

Peter Malanczuk, *Akehurst's Modern Introduction to International Law* (8th rev. ed. 2019).

"Manage Your Citations," UC Berkeley Library, https://guides.lib.berkeley.edu/publichealth/citations.

Max Planck Encyclopedia of Comparative Constitutional Law, https://oxcon.ouplaw.com/ (subscription database).

Max Planck Encyclopedias of International Law, https://opil.ouplaw.com/home/mpil (subscription database). This reference work includes two encyclopedias: the Max Planck Encyclopedia of Public International Law (available in print but not updated) and the Max Planck Encyclopedia of International Procedural Law.

Max Planck Institute for Comparative Public Law and International Law Catalog, https://www.mpil.de/en/pub/library/research-tools.cfm.

Max Planck Yearbook of United Nations Law (1998–). Available on HeinOnline (subscription database).

Stephen Mayeaux, "Bite-Sized Legal Research Tutorial: Foreign Legal Gazettes Guide," https://blogs.loc.gov/law/2024/07/bite-sized-legal-research-tutorial-foreign-legal-gazettes-guide/.

Mendeley, https://www.mendeley.com/.

MICT/ICTR/ICTY Case Law Database, https://www.irmct.org/en.

Mondaq, https://www.mondaq.com/.

Moore, *Digest of International Law* (1906). Available on HeinOnline (subscription database).

Julian Davis Mortenson, "The Meaning of "Investment": ICSID's *Travaux* and the Domain of International Investment Law," 51 *Harvard Int'l L.J.* 257 (2010).

Multilateral Treaties Deposited with the Secretary General (1982–), https://treaties.un.org/.

Multilaw Global Guides, available on Lexis.

Multinational Sources Compared: A Subject and Jurisdiction Index (2021). Available on HeinOnline (subscription database).

Sean Murphy, *United States Practice in International Law* (2002–).

MyCase Blog, Catherine Brock, April 24, 2024, "Legal ChatGPT: Tips, Prompts, and Use Cases," https://www.mycase.com/blog/ai/chatgpt-for-lawyers/.

National Bureau of Economic Research (NBER), Working Papers, https://www.nber.org/papers?page=1&perPage=50&sortBy=public_date.

Netherlands Yearbook of International Law (1970–).

Neue Juristische Wochenschrift (NJW) (1947–) [Germany]. Available on Beck-Online (subscription database).

New Zealand Legal Information Institute (NZLII), http://www.nzlii.org/.

Noble's Revised International Guide to the Law Reports (2002).

"Non Governmental Organizations (NGOs)." UC Berkeley Library, https://guides.lib.berkeley.edu/NGOs.

Notion, https://www.notion.so/notes.

Obsidian, https://obsidian.md/.

OCLC (the Online Computer Library Center), https://www.oclc.org/en/home.html (subscription database).

OECD iLibrary, https://www.oecd-ilibrary.org/.

Official Document System (ODS), https://documents.un.org/.

Official Journal of the European Union, https://eur-lex.europa.eu/oj/direct-access.html.

OPCW Legislation Compendium, https://www.opcw.org/our-work/national-implementation/implementing-legislation/legislation-database/.

OpenAI Platform, "Prompt Engineering Guide," https://platform.openai.com/docs/guides/prompt-engineering.

Open Content Alliance, https://archive.org/details/opencontentalliance.

Opinio Juris, https://opiniojuris.org/.

Oppenheim's International Law: United Nations (Rosalyn Higgins et al., 2017).

ORCID, https://orcid.org/.

Organization of American States, *Treaty Series* (1956–), https://www.oas.org/en/sla/dil/treaties_agreements.asp.

Sabrina Ortiz, "The Best AI Search Engines of 2024: Google, Perplexity, and More," May 7, 2024, https://www.zdnet.com/article/best-ai-search-engine/.

OSCOLA: Oxford University Standard for the Citation of Legal Authorities (4th ed. 2012), https://www.law.ox.ac.uk/oscola.

Oxford Bibliographies: International Law, https://www.oxfordbibliographies.com/ (subscription database). For a quick overview of the subjects covered, see https://www.oxfordbibliographies.com/page/163.

Oxford Constitutions of the World, https://oxcon.ouplaw.com/ (subscription database).

Oxford Encyclopedia of EU Law (OEEUL) (2023–), https://opil.ouplaw.com/home/OEEUL. Available on Oxford Public International Law (subscription database).

The Oxford Guide to Treaties (Duncan B. Hollis, ed., 2nd ed. 2020).

Oxford Handbook of Comparative Law (Mathias Reimann & Rienhard Zimmermann, eds., 2nd ed. 2019). Included in Oxford Handbooks Online (subscription database), https://academic.oup.com/oxford-handbooks-online.

The Oxford Handbook of Constitutional Law in Asia (David S. Law, Holning Lau & Alex Schwartz, eds., 2023). Included in Oxford Handbooks Online (subscription database), https://academic.oup.com/oxford-handbooks-online.

The Oxford Handbook of the Sources of International Law (Samantha Besson & Jean d'Aspremont, eds., 2018). Included in Oxford Handbooks Online (subscription database), https://academic.oup.com/oxford-handbooks-online.

The Oxford Handbook on the United Nations (Thomas G. Weiss, Sam Daws, eds., 2018). Included in Oxford Handbooks Online (subscription database), https://academic.oup.com/oxford-handbooks-online.

Oxford International Organizations (OXIO), https://opil.ouplaw.com/home/OXIO (subscription database).

Oxford Principles of European Union Law (Professor Robert Schütze & Professor Takis Tridimas, eds., 2018).

Oxford Reports on International Law, https://opil.ouplaw.com/home/oril (subscription database).

Oxford Scholarly Authorities Online, https://opil.ouplaw.com/home/OSAIL (subscription database).

Oxford University Press Journals, https://academic.oup.com/journals/ (subscription database).

Pacific Legal Information Institute PacLII (Pacific Islands), http://www.paclii.org/.

PAIS Index, https://proquest.libguides.com/pais (subscription database).

Parry & Grant Encyclopaedic Dictionary of International Law (3rd ed. 2009). Available on Oxford Reference, https://www.oxfordreference.com/ (subscription database).

Peace Palace Library Catalogue, https://peacepalacelibrary.nl/.

Jeffrey S. Peake, "The Decline of Treaties? Obama, Trump, and the Politics of International Agreements" (April 6, 2018). Available at SSRN: https://ssrn.com/abstract=3153840 or http://dx.doi.org/10.2139/ssrn.3153840.

Perma.cc, https://perma.cc/.

Permanent Court of Arbitration, https://pca-cpa.org/en/home/.

Permanent Court of Arbitration Case Repository, https://pca-cpa.org/en/cases/.

Permanent Court of International Justice (PCIJ), https://www.icj-cij.org/en/pcij.

Perplexity, https://www.perplexity.ai/.

The Persistent Objector Rule in International Law (2016).

PowerNotes, https://www.powernotes.com/.

Practical Guidance, available on Lexis.

Practical Law, available on Westlaw.

The Practice and Procedure of the Inter-American Court of Human Rights (2nd ed. 2013).

Jonathan Pratter, "*À la Recherche des Travaux Préparatoires*: An Approach to Researching the Drafting History of International Agreements," https://www.nyulawglobal.org/globalex/Travaux_Preparatoires1.html.

Project Gutenberg, https://www.gutenberg.org/.

Project Muse, https://muse.jhu.edu/ (subscription database).

Donald Raistrick, *Index to Legal Citations and Abbreviations* (4th ed. 2013).

Refworks, https://proquest.libguides.com/refworks (subscription database).

RefWorld (UNHCR), https://www.refworld.org/.

RefWorld, Case Law Collection, https://www.refworld.org/collections/case-law.

Register of Commission Documents, European Commission, https://ec.europa.eu/transparency/documents-register/.

"Report of the International Law Commission to the General Assembly (Part II): Ways and Means of Making the Evidence of Customary International Law More Readily Available," [1950] 2 *Y.B. Int'l L. Comm'n* 367, ILC Doc. A/1316, https://legal.un.org/ilc/documentation/english/reports/a_cn4_34.pdf.

Research Handbook on International Procedural Law (Joanna Gomula, Stephan Wittich & Markus Stemeseder, eds., 2024).

Restatement of the Law, Fourth, the Foreign Relations Law of the United States (2018, annual supplements). Available on Lexis, Westlaw, and HeinOnline.

Restatement of the Law, Third, Foreign Relations (1987–, annual supplement). Available on Lexis, Westlaw, and HeinOnline.

Peter Robinson Summaries of Decisions (Digests), https://peterrobinson.com/digests/.

Shabtai Rosenne, *Practice and Methods of International Law* (1984).

Shabtai Rosenne, *Rosenne's Law and Practice of the International Court: 1920–2015* (5th ed.

2016). Available on Brill Online, https://brill.com/view/db/rose (subscription database).

Russian Yearbook of International Law (1994–).

Renu Urvashi Sagreiya, "Researching Customary International Law, State Practice, and the Pronouncements of States Regarding International Law" (2024). https://www.nyulawglobal.org/globalex/customary_international_law1.html.

S.M.A. Salman, *A Human Rights to Water: Legal and Policy Dimensions* (2004).

William A. Schabas, *Universal Declaration of Human Rights: The Travaux Préparatoires* (2013).

Kirsten Schmalenbach, "International Organizations or Institutions, General Aspects," in *Max Planck Encyclopedias of International Law* (2020), https://opil.ouplaw.com/home (subscription database).

ScholarCheck (HeinOnline), https://libguides.heinonline.org/scholarcheck/overview (subscription database).

ScholarRank (HeinOnline), https://home.heinonline.org/tools/author-profile-pages/scholarrank/ and https://help.heinonline.org/kb/how-is-scholarrank-determined/.

Search Engine Journal, "23 Great Search Engines You Can Use Instead of Google," February 12,

2024, https://www.searchenginejournal.com/alternative-search-engines/271409/#close.

Selected Judgments of the Supreme Court of Israel (1962–). Available on HeinOnline.

Senate Treaty Document Series (formerly the *Senate Executive Document Series)*, https://www.congress.gov/treaties.

Malcolm N. Shaw, *International Law* (9th ed. 2021).

Ilia Maria Siatitsa & Maia Titberidze, "Human Rights in Armed Conflict: Ten Years of Affirmative State Practice within United Nations Resolutions," 3 *J. Int'l Humanitarian Legal Stud.* 233 (2012), https://doi.org/10.1163/18781527-00302007.

Bruno Simma, *Charter of the United Nations: A Commentary* (3rd ed. 2012).

Singapore Statutes Online, https://sso.agc.gov.sg/.

Smit & Herzog on the Law of the European Union (2nd ed. 2010–). Available on Lexis.

Social Science Research Network (SSRN), https://ssrn.com/en/.

Social Science Research Network (SSRN), Top 3,000 Law Authors, https://hq.ssrn.com/rankings/Ranking_Display.cfm?TMY_gID=2&TRN_gID=6.

Sources of State Practice in International Law (2nd rev. ed. 2014).

Southern African Legal Information Institute SAFLII (Southern and Eastern Africa), https://www.saflii.org/.

Spanish Yearbook of International Law (1994–). Available on https://www.sybil.es/sybil/index, Brill Online (vols. 1–17) and HeinOnline (subscription databases).

Special Court for Sierra Leone, https://www.rscsl.org/.

State Practice Regarding State Immunities (2006).

The Statute of the International Court of Justice: A Commentary (Andreas Zimmermann et al., eds., 3rd ed. 2019).

Statutes at Large (1789–), https://www.govinfo.gov/app/collection/STATUTE.

Swedish Statutes in Translation, https://www.government.se/government-policy/judicial-system/swedish-statutes-in-translation--judicial-system/.

Swiss Institute of Comparative Law Catalogue, https://www.isdc.ch/en/library/catalogue-classification.

Daniel Thürer, "Soft Law," in *Max Planck Encyclopedias of International Law* (2009), https://opil.ouplaw.com/home. (subscription database).

Dire Tladi, "Ius Cogens," in *Max Planck Encyclopedias of International Law* (2024), https://opil.ouplaw.com (subscription database).

Joe P. Trachtman, "The Obsolescence of Customary International Law" (October 21, 2014). Available at SSRN: https://ssrn.com/abstract=2512757 or http://dx.doi.org/10.2139/ssrn.2512757.

TradeLawGuide, https://www.tradelawguide.com (subscription database).

Treaties and Other International Acts Series (T.I.A.S) (1946–2016), https://www.state.gov/tias/.

Treaties and Other International Agreements of the United States of America, 1776–1949 (1968–1976), https://www.loc.gov/law/help/us-treaties/bevans.php.

Treaties and Other International Agreements: The Role of the United States Senate: A Study, prepared for the Committee on Foreign Relations, United States Senate, S. Print 106–71 (2001), https://www.govinfo.gov/content/pkg/CPRT-106SPRT66922/pdf/CPRT-106SPRT66922.pdf.

Treaties in Force, https://www.state.gov/treaties-in-force/. Available on HeinOnline.

Tullio Treves, "Customary International Law," in *Max Planck Encyclopedias of International Law* (2006), https://opil.ouplaw.com/home/mpil (subscription database).

Takis Tridimas, *The Foundations of European Union Law* (9th ed. 2024).

U.K. Legislation, https://www.legislation.gov.uk/.

UN-iLibrary, https://www.un-ilibrary.org/ (subscription database; some content is open access).

United Kingdom's Foreign, Commonwealth & Development Office, https://www.gov.uk/government/organisations/foreign-commonwealth-development-office.

United Kingdom Treaty Series (1982–), https://treaties.fco.gov.uk/responsive/app/consolidatedSearch/.

United Nations, https://www.un.org/en/.

United Nations, Ask DAG, https://ask.un.org/.

United Nations Assistance to the Khmer Rouge Trials (UNAKRT), https://www.unakrt-online.org.

United Nations, Audiovisual Library of International Law, https://legal.un.org/avl/intro/welcome_avl.html.

United Nations Charter, https://www.un.org/en/about-us/un-charter.

United Nations Conference on Trade and Development (UNCTAD) International Investment Agreements Navigator, https://investmentpolicy.unctad.org/international-investment-agreements.

United Nations Convention on Contracts for the International Sale of Goods (CISG), https://iicl.law.pace.edu/cisg/cisg.

United Nations, Dag Hammarskjöld Library, https://www.un.org/library.

United Nations, Dag Hammarskjöld Library, Research Guides, https://research.un.org/en. This site includes all the research guides cited in Chapter 8.

United Nations, Documents, https://www.un.org/en/sections/general/documents/.

United Nations, Economic and Social Council, https://ecosoc.un.org/en.

United Nations Framework Convention on Climate Change, https://unfccc.int/.

United Nations, General Assembly, https://www.un.org/en/ga/.

United Nations High Commissioner for Human Rights, International Human Rights Law, https://www.ohchr.org/en/instruments-and-mechanisms/international-human-rights-law.

United Nations International Law Commission, https://legal.un.org/ilc/.

United Nations International Law Commission, Global Search, https://legal.un.org/globalsearch/dtSearch/Search_Forms/dtSearch.html.

United Nations International Law Commission, *Yearbook of the International Law Commission* (1949–), https://legal.un.org/ilc/publications/yearbooks/.

United Nations Law Collection. Available on HeinOnline (subscription database).

United Nations, Multilateral Treaties Deposited with the Secretary General, https://treaties.un.org/pages/participationstatus.aspx?clang=_en.

United Nations Office on Drugs and Crime (UNODC), Laws on Crime, https://sherloc.unodc.org/cld/en/st/home.html.

United Nations, Official Document System (ODS), https://documents.un.org/.

United Nations, Secretariat, https://www.un.org/en/about-us/secretariat.

United Nations, Secretary-General, https://www.un.org/sg/en.

United Nations, Security Council, https://main.un.org/securitycouncil/en.

United Nations Security Council, Voting System, https://www.un.org/securitycouncil/content/voting-system.

United Nations, Specialized Agencies and Other Programs, https://www.un.org/en/about-us/un-system.

United Nations Treaty Collection, https://treaties.un.org/.

United Nations, *Treaty Handbook* (rev. ed. 2013), https://treaties.un.org/Pages/Resource.aspx?path=Publication/TH/Page1_en.xml.

United Nations Treaty Series (1947–), https://treaties.un.org/. Available on HeinOnline (subscription database).

United Nations, Trusteeship Council, https://www.un.org/en/about-us/trusteeship-council.

United Nations, UN Digital Library, https://digitallibrary.un.org/.

U.S. Department of Commerce, Trade and Related Agreements Database, https://www.trade.gov/all-trade-agreements.

U.S. Department of State, https://www.state.gov/.

U.S. Income Tax Treaties, https://www.irs.gov/businesses/international-businesses/united-states-income-tax-treaties-a-to-z.

U.S. Trade Representative, https://ustr.gov/trade-agreements.

U.S. Treaties and Agreements Library. Available on HeinOnline (subscription database).

United States Treaties and Other International Agreements (U.S.T.) (1950–1984). Available on HeinOnline (subscription database).

United States Treaty Index (I. Kavass, ed., 1991–). Available on HeinOnline (subscription database).

Jorge A. Vargas, *Mexican Legal Dictionary* (2009–2010).

The Vienna Convention on the Law of Treaties: A Commentary (Olivier Corten & Pierre Klein, eds.) (2011).

vLex, https://vlex.com/ (subscription database).

vLex, "Developing the Future of Legal AI," https://vmeo.com/985710964.

vLex, "Whitepaper: LLMs for Legal Tasks," February 7, 2024, https://vlex.com/blog/whitepaper-generativeai.

Gerhard von Glahn & James Larry Taulbee, *Law Among Nations: An Introduction to Public International Law* (11th ed. 2017).

Yilin Wang, "The Origins and Operation of the General Principles of Law as Gap Fillers," 13 *J. Int'l Dispute Settlement* 560–582 (2022), https://doi.org/10.1093/jnlids/idac018.

War Crimes Prosecution Watch, https://www.publicinternationallawandpolicygroup.org/war-crime-watch.

Washington and Lee Law Journal Rankings, https://managementtools4.wlu.edu/LawJournals/.

Alan Watson, *Comparative Law: Law, Reality and Society* (3rd ed. 2010).

Westlaw, http://westlaw.com (subscription database).

West's Law and Commercial Dictionary in Five Languages: Definitions of the Legal and Commercial Terms and Phrases of American, English and Civil Law Jurisdictions (1985).

Wharton, *Digest of the International Law of the United States* (1886). Available on HeinOnline (subscription database).

Whiteman, *Digest of International Law* (1963–1973). Available on HeinOnline (subscription database).

Christian L. Wiktor, *Multilateral Treaty Calendar = Répertoire des Traités Multilatéraux, 1648–1995* (1998). Available on HeinOnline (subscription database).

WIPOLex, https://www.wipo.int/en/web/wipolex.

Jennifer (Greig) Wondracek, "Introducing AI Prompt Worksheets for the Legal Profession," January 22, 2024, https://www.llrx.com/2024/01/introducing-ai-prompt-worksheets-for-the-legal-profession/.

World Bank Open Knowledge Repository, https://openknowledge.worldbank.org/home.

WorldCat, https://search.worldcat.org/.

World Constitutions Illustrated. Available on HeinOnline (subscription database).

World Court Practice Guide: Summaries and Index of PCIJ and ICJ Cases (Inna Uchkunova, ed., 2016).

Worldcourts, https://worldcourts.com/.

World Dictionary of Legal Abbreviations (1991–).

WorldLII, http://www.worldlii.org.

WorldLII Countries, http://www.worldlii.org/countries.html.

WorldLII Courts & Case-Law, http://www.worldlii.org/catalog/2172.html.

WorldLII International Courts & Tribunals Project, http://www.worldlii.org/int/cases.

WorldLII International Legal Scholarship Library, http://www.worldlii.org/int/journals/.

WorldLII International Treaties Collection, http://www.worldlii.org/int/special/treaties/.

World Trade Law, https://www.worldtradelaw.net/ (subscription database).

World Trade Organization (WTO), https://www.wto.org/.

WTO Organization Chart, https://www.wto.org/english/thewto_e/whatis_e/tif_e/org2_e.htm.

World Trade Organization (WTO), Dispute Settlement, https://www.wto.org/english/tratop_e/dispu_e/dispu_e.htm.

World Trade Organization (WTO), Documents Online, https://docs.wto.org/dol2fe/Pages/FE_Search/FE_S_S005.aspx.

Worldwide Political Science Abstracts, https://proquest.libguides.com/wpsa (subscription database).

WPCW Legislation Compendium, https://www.opcw.org/resources/national-implementation/legislation-compendium.

"WTO/GATT Research," NYU Law Library, https://nyulaw.libguides.com/wto_gatt.

Yearbook of International Environmental Law (1990–). Available on Oxford Academic Journals, https://academic.oup.com/yielaw/ (subscription database).

Yearbook of International Organizations (1967–). Available on Brill Online, https://ybio.brillonline.com/ (subscription database). Limited freely available information is available at https://uia.org/ybio/. (subscription database).

Yearbook of the United Nations (1946/47–), https://www.un.org/en/yearbook and https://www.un.org/en/yearbook/prepress.

Marcus Zillman, "Deep Web Research and Discovery Resources," https://deepweb.us/.

Marcus Zillman, "Guide to Searching the Internet," https://www.searchingtheinternet.info/.

Zotero, https://www.zotero.org/.

"Zotero for Law Students and Scholars," Washington and Lee Law Library, https://libguides.wlu.edu/c.php?g=99586&p=644177.

"Zotero Research Guide," UC Berkeley Library, https://guides.lib.berkeley.edu/zotero.

APPENDIX B

WEBSITES CONTAINING NATIONAL LAW

A. TRANSLATED LAWS

In addition to the sources mentioned in Chapter 3, see the following sites for access to translated national law. All of these sites are freely available and contain many translations. However, in some cases, there may be only a few translations. See also Jennifer Allison, "Foreign Law—Subject Law Collections on the Web," for more websites and databases by subject (with and without translations).[1]

Subject Collections

African Human Rights Case Law Analyser
https://caselaw.ihrda.org/.

Animal Welfare Legislation Database (AWLD)
https://www.globalanimallaw.org/database/.

Constitute Project, World Constitutions
https://www.constituteproject.org.

Data Protection Laws of the World (DLA Piper)
https://www.dlapiperdataprotection.com.

Death Penalty Worldwide
https://www.deathpenaltyworldwide.org/.

---

[1] https://www.nyulawglobal.org/globalex/foreign_collections1.html.

ECOLEX
National environmental law.
https://www.ecolex.org.

Electoral Knowledge Network (Ace Project)
https://aceproject.org/regions-en (election laws).

FAOLEX (FAO)
National laws and regulations on food, agriculture, and renewable natural resources. Also available from the FAO: Family Farming Lex, FishLex, and legislation on pastoralism. https://www.fao.org/faolex/en.

Freedom of Information Database (freedominfo.org)
https://www.freedominfo.org/regions/.

Global Database on Violence Against Women (UN Women)
https://data.unwomen.org/evaw/database.

Global Data Protection, Privacy & Surveillance Law Library
http://www.worldlii.org/int/special/privacy/.

Global Freedom of Expression
Caselaw on freedom of expression and information.
https://globalfreedomofexpression.columbia.edu.

Global Health and Human Rights
https://www.globalhealthrights.org/.

Global Insolvency Law Database (World Bank)
https://www.worldbank.org/en/topic/financialsector/brief/global-insolvency-law-database.

International Center for Non-Profit, Digital Legal Library
https://www.icnl.org/resources/library.

Juricaf
Jurisprudence from Francophone countries.
https://juricaf.org/recherche.

Legislationonline.org (OSCE)
Legislation dealing with the rule of law, human rights and fundamental freedoms.
https://www.legislationline.org.

Maritime Space: Maritime Zones and Maritime Delimitation
https://www.un.org/depts/los/LEGISLATIONANDTREATIES/.

National Implementation of International Humanitarian Law (ICRC)
https://ihl-databases.icrc.org/en/national-practice/national-implementation-of-ihl.

NATLEX—Database of National Labor Social Security and Related Human Rights Legislation (ILO)
https://natlex.ilo.org/dyn/natlex2/r/natlex/fe/home.

REFWORLD (UNHCR)
Law relating to refugees, asylum seekers, stateless persons.
https://www.refworld.org/.

UNODC, SHERLOC
Legislation and Case Law on Crime and Terrorism.
https://sherloc.unodc.org/cld/en/st/home.html.

UrbanLex (UN Habitat)
A collection of policies, laws, decisions and practices that govern the management and development of the urban environment.
https://urbanlex.unhabitat.org.

WIPO Lex: Access to Legal Information on Intellectual Property from Around the World
https://www.wipo.int/en/web/wipolex/index.

Women & Justice Collection
https://www.law.cornell.edu/women-and-justice.

World Trade Organization
(Good source for laws associated with trade topics, see the trade topics page and the official documents database)
https://www.wto.org/.

Individual Countries/Regions

This is not a comprehensive list, so check out the research guides and other sources noted in Chapter 3. See also "Country by Country Guide to Foreign Law

Research" (Yale Law Library)[2] or other research guides for more national law databases.

AsianLII
http://www.asianlii.org/.

AustLII (Australia)
https://www.austlii.edu.au/.

BAILII (UK and Ireland)
https://www.bailii.org/.

CanLII (Canada)
https://www.canlii.org/.

CommonLII (The Commonwealth)
http://www.commonlii.org/.

Estonian Legislation in English
https://www.riigiteataja.ee/en/.

Finlex (Finland)
https://www.finlex.fi/en/.

Foreign Law Translations (Austria, France, Germany, Israel)
https://law.utexas.edu/transnational/foreign-law-translations/.

Gesetze im Internet, German Law on the Internet
https://www.gesetze-im-internet.de/Teilliste_translations.html.

---

2 https://library.law.yale.edu/research-guides/country-country-guide-foreign-legal-research.

HKLII (Hong Kong)
https://www.hklii.org/.

Hong Kong, Bilingual Laws Information System
https://www.elegislation.gov.hk.

Japanese Law Translation
https://www.japaneselawtranslation.go.jp/.

Legal Information System of the Republic of Austria
https://www.ris.bka.gv.at/Englische-Rv/.

Legal Information System of Regulatory Legal Acts of the Republic of Kazakhstan
https://adilet.zan.kz/eng/index/docs.

Lovdata in English (Norway)
https://lovdata.no/info/information_in_english.

NZLII (New Zealand)
https://www.nzlii.org/.

PacLII (Pacific Islands)
http://www.paclii.org/.

SAFLII (Southern Africa)
https://www.saflii.org/.

Singapore Statutes Online
https://sso.agc.gov.sg.

Swedish Statutes in Translation
https://www.government.se/government-policy/judicial-system/swedish-statutes-in-translation--judicial-system/.

Vietnam Laws
https://www.vietnamlaws.com/vietnamlawsonline_freeversion.aspx.

B. SUBSCRIPTION DATABASES—INDIVIDUAL COUNTRIES, REGIONS, COMPARATIVE

This is not a comprehensive list, so check out the research guides and other sources noted in Chapter 3. Foreign Law Guide is a good source for information about country-specific subscription databases. Some of the databases contain laws in the vernacular and in English translation. See also the NYU Law Library research guide, "Foreign Law by Jurisdiction."[3]

Note that both Lexis and Westlaw have country-specific versions with national law in the vernacular. Check with your law librarian for more information.

Asia
Westlaw Asia
https://www.westlawasia.com.

Australia
Lexis Australia
https://www.lexisnexis.com.au/en/homepage.
Jade Professional
https://jade.io/j/?a=go_pro.
Lawlex
https://lawlex.com.au.

---

[3] https://nyulaw.libguides.com/foreign-law.

Westlaw Australia
https://www.thomsonreuters.com.au/en-au/products/westlaw.html.

Austria
Lexis Austria.
https://www.lexisnexis.at/.
RDB
https://rdb.manz.at/.

Belgium
Jurisquare
https://jurisquare.be/fr/index.html.
LegalWorld (Wolters Kluwer)
https://www.wolterskluwer.com/nl-be/know/legalworld.
Strada Lex
https://www.stradalex.com.

Canada
Centre d'accès à l'information juridique (CAIJ)
https://www.caij.qc.ca.
LexisAdvance Quicklaw
https://www.lexisnexis.ca/en-ca/products/lexis-advance-quicklaw-overview.page.
WestlawNext Canada
https://www.westlawnextcanada.com.

China
Chinese Local Gazetteers Database
https://fz.wanfangdata.com.cn/.
LawInfoChina (PKULaw China)
https://www.pkulaw.com/.
Lexis China
https://www.lexiscn.com/en/.

Commonwealth of Independent States (CIS) & Russia
(Armenia, Azerbaijan, Belarus, Kazakhstan, Kyrgyzstan, Moldova, Russia, Tajikistan, Turkmenistan, Uzbekistan, Ukraine)
CIS Legislation
https://cis-legislation.com/.

Congo
Codes Larcier de la République démocratique du Congo
https://clrdc.larcier.com/homedir/index.php.

Gulf Legislation Network (Bahrain, Emirates, Kuwait, Oman, Qatar, Saudi Arabia)
https://gulflegislation.com/default.Aspx.

France
Dalloz
https://www.dalloz.fr/.
Lamyline
https://www.lamyline.fr/Content/Search.aspx.
LeDoctrinal
https://www.doctrinal.fr/.
Lexbase
https://www.lexbase.fr/.
Lexis France
https://www.lexisnexis.com/fr-fr.
Lextenso
https://www.labase-lextenso.fr/?.

Germany
Beck-Online
https://beck-online.beck.de/Home.

Jurion (Wolters Kluwer)
https://research.wolterskluwer-online.de/bibliothek.
Juris
https://www.juris.de/jportal/nav/index.jsp#/.
Lexis Germany
https://www.lexisnexis.com/de-de.

India
Manupatra
https://www.manupatrafast.com/.

SCC Online
https://www.scconline.com/web-edition.

Italy
DeJure—Giuffre
https://dejure.it/#/home.
Diritto Giustizia
https://www.dirittoegiustizia.it/#/.

Liechtenstein
Recht Portal für Liechtenstein
https://www.rechtportal.li/default.aspx?m=583.

Luxembourg
Strad Lex Luxembourg
https://www.stradalex.lu.

Middle East and North Africa (MENA)
Lexis Middle East
https://www.lexis.ae.
Westlaw Middle East and North Africa
https://mena.thomsonreuters.com/en/products-services/legal/westlaw.html.

Morocco
Artemis
https://www.artemis.ma/accueil.

Pakistan
PakistanLawSite
http://www.pakistanlawsite.com/.

Poland
LEX
https://www.lex.pl.

Russia
CIS Legislation
https://cis-legislation.com/.

GARANT
http://english.garant.ru/.

Scandinavia
Lovdata (Norway)
https://lovdata.no/.
Norstedts Juridik (Sweden)
https://www.nj.se.

Singapore
LawNet
https://www.lawnet.sg/lawnet/web/lawnet/home.

South Africa
Juta Law (Namibie, Tanzanie, Zambie & Zimbabwe)
https://juta.co.za/.

Spain
Westlaw Spain (Aranzadi)
http://www.aranzadidigital.es/.

Switzerland
SwissLex
https://www.swisslex.ch.
Weblaw
http://www.weblaw.ch/.
ZPO/CPC Online
https://app.zpo-cpc.ch/users/sign_in.

United Kingdom
ICLR
https://www.iclr.co.uk.
Lexis UK
https://www.lexisnexis.co.uk/.
vLex
https://vlex.com/.
Westlaw UK
https://legalsolutions.thomsonreuters.co.uk/en/products-services/westlaw-uk.html.

Comparative
Global Regulation
https://www.global-regulation.com/.
LLMC Digital (primarily archival collections)
https://llmc.com.
vLex
https://vlex.com/.

APPENDIX C

TREATY COLLECTIONS

Many electronic treaty collections are included in this Appendix. However, not every collection is included herein. For more information on locating treaties, see Chapter 4.

General Collections

Flare Index to Treaties
https://resources.ials.sas.ac.uk/digital/ials-digital-resources/flare-index-treaties.

Oxford Historical Treaties
https://opil.ouplaw.com/home/OHT
(subscription database).

United Nations Law Collection (HeinOnline)
https://home.heinonline.org/ (subscription database).

United Nations Treaty Collection
https://treaties.un.org/.

WorldLII, International Treaties Collection
http://www.worldlii.org/int/special/treaties/.

World Treaty Library (HeinOnline)
https://home.heinonline.org/ (subscription database).

Topic-Specific Collections or Collections by Issuing Body / Organization

African Union / OAU Treaties. Conventions, Protocols & Charters
https://au.int/en/treaties.

Australian Treaties Database
https://info.dfat.gov.au/TREATIES.

Australian Treaties Library
https://www.austlii.edu.au/au/other/dfat/.

Avalon Project (Yale Law School)
https://avalon.law.yale.edu/default.asp.

Bilateral Investment Treaties (UNCTAD)
https://investmentpolicy.unctad.org/international-investment-agreements.

Council of Europe, European Treaties
https://www.coe.int/en/web/conventions/full-list.

ECOLEX (international environmental law)
https://www.ecolex.org/.

EUR-Lex (EU Treaties)
https://eur-lex.europa.eu/collection/eu-law/treaties/treaties-force.html.

FAOLEX (FAO)
https://www.fao.org/legal/databases/faolex/en/.

Hague Conventions on Private International Law
https://www.hcch.net/en/instruments/conventions.

Hong Kong Treaties (HKLII)
https://www.hklii.hk/en/legis/hkts/.

IAEA Treaties
https://www.iaea.org/resources/legal/treaties.

ICAO Treaty Collection
https://www.icao.int/secretariat/legal/pages/trea tycollection.aspx.

International Bureau of Fiscal Documentation (IBFD), Tax Treaties
https://www.ibfd.org/ (subscription database).

International Humanitarian Law Database (ICRC)
https://www.icrc.org/en/icrc-databases-international-humanitarian-law.

International Investment Agreements Navigator (UNCTAD)
https://investmentpolicy.unctad.org/international-investment-agreements.

Kluwer Arbitration, Multilateral Treaties
https://www.kluwerarbitration.com (subscription database).

Ministère de L'Europe et des Affaires Etrangères, France Diplomatie (Treaties with France as party) https://www.diplomatie.gouv.fr/fr/photos-videos-publications-infographies/bases-documentaires/ (French-language resource).

New York Convention Secretariat (UNCITRAL)
https://uncitral.un.org/.

NORMLEX (ILO)
https://normlex.ilo.org/dyn/normlex/en/f?p=NORMLEXPUB:1:0::NO:::.

OECD, Tax Treaties
https://www.oecd.org/en/topics/tax-treaties.html.

Organization of American States (OAS) Treaties
https://www.oas.org/en/topics/treaties_agreements.asp.

Treaties in Force (U.S.)
https://www.state.gov/treaties-in-force/.

UK Treaties Online
https://treaties.fcdo.gov.uk/responsive/app/consolidatedSearch/.

United Nations, Human Rights Instruments (UNHCHR) (core and universal instruments)
https://www.ohchr.org/en/instruments-listings.

United Nations Office of Counter-Terrorism, International Legal Instruments
https://www.un.org/counterterrorism/international-legal-instruments.

United Nations Office on Drugs and Crime (UNODC), SHERLOC Treaties Database
https://sherloc.unodc.org/cld/v3/sherloc/treaties/index.html?lng=en#?mv=signatures&v=results.

United Nations Treaty Collection
https://treaties.un.org/Pages/Home.aspx.

United States Congress, Treaty Documents
https://www.congress.gov/search?q=%7B%22source%22%3A%22treaties%22%7D.

United States Department of the Treasury Resource Center (U.S. tax treaties)
https://home.treasury.gov/policy-issues/tax-policy/treaties.

United States Library of Congress, Treaties
https://www.loc.gov/collections/united-states-treaties-and-other-international-agreements/about-this-collection/.

United States Senate, Treaties
https://www.senate.gov/legislative/treaties_new.htm.

United States Senate Committee on Foreign Relations, Treaties
https://www.foreign.senate.gov/activities-and-reports/treaties.

United States Trade Representative, Free Trade Agreements
https://ustr.gov/trade-agreements/free-trade-agreements.

University of Minnesota Human Rights Library
http://hrlibrary.umn.edu/.

World Intellectual Property Organization, WIPO Administered Treaties
https://www.wipo.int/treaties/en/.

World Intellectual Property Organization, WIPO Lex, Treaties Collection https://www.wipo.int/wipolex/en/main/treaties.

World Trade Organization Legal Texts https://www.wto.org/english/docs_e/legal_e/legal_e.htm.

INDEX

References are to Pages
